MODERN PATCHWORK HOME

DYNAMIC QUILTS & PROJECTS FOR EVERY ROOM

Edited by

VIVIKA HANSEN DENEGRE

EDITORIAL DIRECTOR
Kerry Bogert

EDITOR
Vivika Hansen DeNegre

CONTENT EDITOR
Jodi Butler

ART DIRECTOR + COVER DESIGNER
Ashlee Wadeson

INTERIOR DESIGNER
Karla Baker

PHOTOGRAPHERS
Hornick Rivlin Studio, Larry Stein, Sharon White Studio, Dean Schoeppner, Jay Wilde

www.fwcommunity.com

22 21 20 19 18 5 4 3 2 1

Modern Courthouse Steps (detail) by Siobhan Rogers

CONTENTS

INTRODUCTION

A dear friend recently asked me why I enjoy modern quilts so much. If that isn't a loaded question for the editor of quilting magazines, I don't know what is! But it got me thinking: I love the aesthetic not only because of the retro vibe and innovative designs but also because modern quilting is the next logical step in the evolution of the craft. We are just on the cusp of the modern revolution. Complex traditional quilt patterns are being reimagined in bold colorways with simplified construction. Modern quilters are honing their design and technical skills by incorporating scale, symmetry, and repetition in ways their foremothers would never have imagined. They are creating their own quilting legacy, and it is amazing to be part of this movement.

But most of all, modern quilts have a practical aspect that appeals to so many contemporary quiltmakers: these quilts are designed to be used. They are not made to be tucked away in a hope chest or hidden behind the doors of a cedar closet. Modern quilts are proudly displayed in homes, carried to outdoor concerts and picnics, gifted for births and graduations, and—if you are brave—laundered (on gentle!) in the washing machine. We live with them, and they are part of our lives.

Modern Patchwork Home shares a curated collection of 24 projects, including accessories like totes and bags, quilted home décor items such as pillows and wall hangings, and a dozen eye-popping quilts. The projects were chosen with the discerning modern sewist in mind: they are innovative, diverse, useful, and on trend. You'll find a variety of projects, from funky kitchen items to sophisticated quilts, perfect for even the most discerning modern quilt enthusiast. And even better, many of the projects are beginner-friendly and would make great gifts.

While you are leafing through the pages, consider your own quilting legacy. What is it about the modern quilt movement that inspires you? How do the quilts and accessories you've made for your own home reflect your design aesthetic? And most importantly, what's next on your design wall?

Best,

Divika

Left: Module Quilt by Christine Barnes.

1

QUILTING BASICS

TECHNIQUES AND TIME-SAVING TIPS FOR THE MODERN QUILTER

Tips to help you get started

- Use ¼" (6 mm) seam allowances unless otherwise noted.

- Stitch with the fabric right sides together.

- After stitching a seam, press to set the seam, and then open the fabrics and press the seam allowance toward the darker fabric.

- Yardages are based upon 40"–wide (101.5 cm) fabric after the selvedges have been removed.

Half-Square Triangle Blocks
TWO AT A TIME

Half-Square Triangle blocks (HSTs) are some of the most common and versatile blocks we use in quilting, but the bias-edge seam makes them a bit of a challenge. This quick method for making two identical HST blocks at one time eliminates the need to sew along a cut bias edge—you get more blocks with less fuss.

1   Cut two squares ⅞" (2.2 cm) larger than the desired finished size of your block.

2   Using a ruler, draw a diagonal line on the wrong side of the lighter square from the upper left to the lower right corner (**Figure 1**).

3   With right sides facing, pair a dark square with the marked light square.

4   Stitch ¼" (6 mm) on each side of the drawn line (**Figure 2**).

5   Cut along the drawn line, creating 2 HSTs (**Figure 3**).

6   Press the seam allowances either open or toward the darker fabric. Trim the dog ears (**Figure 4**).

7   Voila! You now have 2 HST blocks to use in your next quilt!

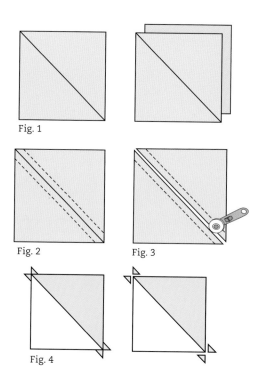

Fig. 1

Fig. 2

Fig. 3

Fig. 4

Make a Block in Any Size

You can make any size HST block with this Two at a Time method by using the following formula:

Cut 2 squares ⅞" (2.2 cm) larger than the desired finished size of the block. For example, to make 2 HST blocks that finish at 4" (10 cm), cut (2) 4⅞" (12.5 cm) squares.

> **NOTE**: *Some quilters cut the blocks 1" (2.5 cm) larger than the desired finished size and then trim the pressed blocks down to the final size. It's a little more work, but these quilters prefer the additional accuracy.*

Half-Square Triangle Blocks
EIGHT AT A TIME

This time-saving method helps you make 8 HSTs at a time—quickly and accurately.

1 Using a ruler, draw diagonal lines on the lighter square from the upper left to lower right and from the upper right to the lower left (**Figure 1**).

2 Draw center vertical and horizontal lines (**Figure 2**).

3 With right sides together, pair a dark square with the marked light square.

4 Stitch ¼" (6 mm) on each side of the diagonal lines only.

5 Cut along the drawn diagonal lines (**Figure 3**), and again at the center vertical and horizontal lines, creating 8 HSTs (**Figure 4**).

6 Press the seam allowances either open or toward the darker fabric. Trim the dog ears (**Figure 5**).

7 Voilà! You now have 8 HST blocks to use in your next quilt!

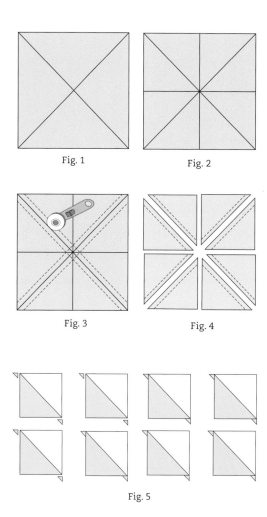

Fig. 1   Fig. 2

Fig. 3   Fig. 4

Fig. 5

Make a Block in Any Size

You can make any size HST block with this Eight at a Time method by using the following formula:

Multiply the measurement of the desired finished HST block by 2, then add 1¾" (4.5 cm). It works every time!

For example, to make 8 HST units with a finished size of 4" (10 cm) square, cut the initial squares at 9¾" (25 cm) square.

$$\textbf{(4" × 2) + 1¾" = 9¾"}$$
$$\textbf{[(10 cm × 2) + 4.5 cm = 25 cm]}$$

Foundation Paper-Piecing

Foundation paper-piecing is a fantastic way to create complicated designs in fabric. If you're not familiar with paper piecing, here's an easy introduction.

1   The shapes on paper-piecing blocks are numbered (**Figure 1**).

2   Using fabric pieces that are larger than the numbered areas, place fabric 1 on the wrong side of the paper, right side up (**Figure 2**).

3   Position fabric 2 on top of fabric 1, right sides facing and edges aligned. Make sure the edges of fabric 2 will extend at least ¼" (6 mm) beyond the printed lines when pressed back into place (**Figure 3**).

4   With the paper on top, stitch directly on the pattern line between pieces 1 and 2, extending the stitching into the seam allowances at the end of the seams (**Figure 4**).

5   Press fabric 2 back. Fold the paper back along the stitched line and trim the seam allowance (**Figure 5**).

6   Continue to add pieces in numerical order.

7   Trim the excess paper and fabric ¼" (6 mm) beyond the outer pattern lines.

8   After the blocks have been joined together, carefully tear off the foundation paper.

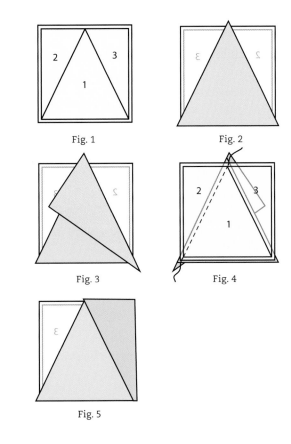

Fig. 1

Fig. 2

Fig. 3

Fig. 4

Fig. 5

Tips for Paper-Piercing

- Print or trace the pattern onto foundation or copy paper. Accuracy matters: Check that the printed patterns are accurate. Sometimes printers and scanners slightly change dimensions; make sure the printed pattern is the same size as the original. You will need one pattern piece for each block.

- Cut the fabric a bit generously. Although it feels wasteful, it will save time and fabric in the long run. We recommend adding ¾" (2 cm) to the piece needed.

- Use a new 90/14 needle and shorten your stitch length to 1.8 mm to make it easier to remove the paper after the quilt is assembled.

- Sewing is done with the paper side up and the fabric beneath. Stitch on the printed lines.

- Make a test block before cutting all of your fabric.

Flying Geese Blocks
FOUR AT A TIME

Flying Geese blocks are made up of the 'Geese,' which is a large, centered triangle in the unit, and the 'Sky' which are the triangles on the sides. There are several ways to make Flying Geese blocks, but if your quilt pattern calls for several in the same color combination, this method can't be beat. There is absolutely no wasted fabric, and no need to work with unstable bias edges. The Geese section begins as a single large square and 4 smaller squares make up the Sky.

1   First, to determine the size of squares to cut, write down the size of the finished block. For our example, we'll use a 2" × 4" (5 cm × 10 cm) finished block.

For the large Geese piece, cut a square the desired finished width of the block plus 1¼" (3.2 cm).

4" + 1¼" = 5¼" square
(10 cm + 3.2 cm = 13.5 cm square)

FOR the smaller Sky pieces, cut 4 squares each the desired finished height of the block plus ⅞" (2.2 cm).

2" + ⅞" = 2⅞" square
(5 cm + 2.2 cm = 7.5 cm square)

2   Draw a diagonal line on the wrong side of 4 Sky (background) squares.

3   Place 1 Sky square on a Geese fabric, right sides together. Place the second Sky square in the opposite corner as shown. Align the raw edges in the corners. The tips of the squares will overlap in the center. Sew ¼" (6 mm) from the drawn line on both sides of the line. Cut on the marked line (**Figure 1**).

4   Press the Sky away from the Geese. You have 2 partial units (**Figure 2**).

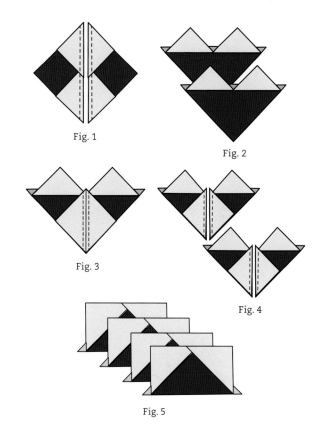

Fig. 1

Fig. 2

Fig. 3

Fig. 4

Fig. 5

5   Working with 1 partial unit at a time, place 1 square with the drawn line perpendicular to the sewn seam, right sides together. Align the raw edges in the corner. Sew ¼" (6 mm) from the drawn line on both sides of the line (**Figure 3**).

6   Cut along the drawn line (**Figure 4**).

7   Press the Sky away from the Geese (**Figure 5**).

8   Repeat with the second partial unit. Voilà, 4 Flying Geese!

Curved Piecing

Curved piecing is ubiquitous in modern quilts, but some quilters ignore it because they've avoided learning how to sew curves. Like many things, piecing curves takes a little practice. With these tips, you'll soon be creating smooth curved seams like a pro!

NOTE: *These illustrations show the Drunkard's Path block but these tips are true for all blocks with curved pieces.*

1 Cut a convex quarter circle piece and a concave L-shaped piece from contrasting fabrics (**Figure 1**). Fold each piece in half. Finger press at the curved centers.

2 With right sides together and the L-shaped piece on top, align press marks and pin in the center of the block (**Figure 2**).

3 Pin the outside edges together with the straight edges matching (**Figure 3**).

4 You might find it necessary to add more pins between the 3 original pins, but this step is optional (**Figure 4**).

5 Sew the curve. Sew slowly and remove the pins as you come to them, easing the top and bottom fabrics together to avoid tucks.

6 Press the seams toward the quarter circle piece to make it pop, or toward the L-shaped piece to make the circles recede. A bit of spray starch helps keep the circles smooth.

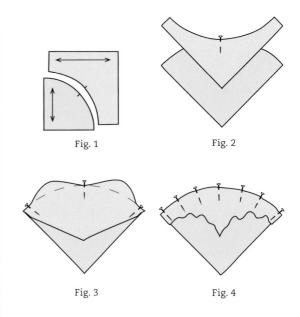

Fig. 1   Fig. 2

Fig. 3   Fig. 4

Accuracy Matters

For curved blocks, precision cutting and sewing will make a difference in piecing success. Here are some tips for troubleshooting them.

SMOOTH CURVES: Always sew with the L-shaped piece on top so you can see the fabric as it eases into the curved shape of the quarter circle as you sew.

OFF-KILTER BLOCKS: If the fabric is pulled when sewing, the block might stretch out of square. Try trimming the block to size, or pick out the stitches, press the pieces with starch, and sew again.

TUCKS: Sometimes small tucks may get sewn into the seam. If this happens, pull out the stitches around the tuck, ease the fabrics back together, and re-sew the open portion with a smooth curve.

SAVE TIME: Making a single block can be time consuming. Batching tasks helps establish a more efficient routine when sewing—cut all the pieces, then move to pinning, sewing, pressing, and finally squaring them all up.

Sew Perfect Y-seams

Patchwork blocks such as Hexagons or Tumbling Blocks have three seams that intersect in a "Y" shape and cannot be assembled with continuous edge-to-edge stitching. Y-seam construction requires starting and stopping ¼" (6 mm) from the edge of the patchwork in order to create blocks that lie flat and do not pucker. The following technique simplifies Y-seam construction to "dot-to-dot" sewing. With a little practice, it will become second nature!

SIMPLE Y-SEAM CONSTRUCTION

1 Using a sharp pen or mechanical pencil, mark the point where the ¼" (6 mm) seam allowances intersect on the wrong side of each piece. This dot indicates where to start and stop sewing (**Figure 1**).

2 Align 2 of the pieces, right sides facing. Sew a seam from "dot to dot" being sure to backstitch at the beginning and end of the seam to lock it in place (**Figure 2**).

3 Open the patchwork and align the next piece in place onto 1 side of the partial block, matching the dots. Sew a seam from dot to dot (**Figure 3**).

4 Pivot the piece and align the last raw edges together. Pin in place. Sew dot to dot. Open and press the block, fanning the seams where they intersect, if desired (**Figure 4**).

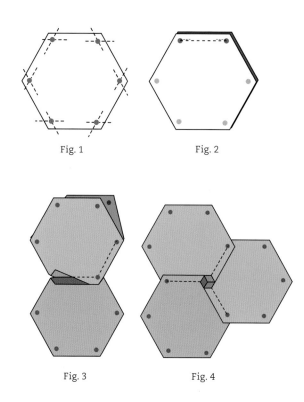

Fig. 1   Fig. 2

Fig. 3   Fig. 4

Tips for Successful Y-seam Construction

- Handle the block components carefully. The pieces contain bias edges and may stretch.

- Always anchor the stitches at the beginning and end of the seam with a few backstitches.

- Precision matters. Sew an accurate ¼" (6 mm) seam and do not sew beyond the dot into the seam allowance. If puckering occurs, pick out any stitches that are in the seam allowances.

- Press the seams in 1 direction (clockwise or counter clockwise) in order to fan the intersection and reduce bulk where the 3 seams meet.

- Practice makes perfect! This is a technique used frequently in Hexagon, Star, Tumbling Block, and other quilt patterns and becomes easier with practice!

Easy Envelope Pillow Backs
WITH OR WITHOUT A BINDING

Use these simple directions to finish pillows with an envelope closure. Binding or no binding? That's up to you.

Materials

Pillow top

Backing fabric

Pillow form

Point turner

Binding strips, 2¼" (5.5 cm) × (the pillow perimeter + 5" [12.5 cm]) (for the Envelope Back with Binding option only)

Fig. 1

Fig. 2

ENVELOPE BACK WITHOUT BINDING

1   Cut 2 pieces of backing fabric, each the height of the finished pillow plus ½" (1.3 cm) (for seam allowances) and the width of the finished pillow plus 6" (15 cm) (for overlap). As an example, for a 16" (40.5 cm) square pillow, cut (2) 22" × 16½" (56 cm × 42 cm) rectangles.

2   Fold and press the rectangles in half widthwise, wrong sides facing. (In our example, the rectangles would be 11" × 16½" [28 cm × 42 cm].)

3   Overlap the pressed edges, making a square the size of the pillow top.

4   Baste the overlapped edges together at the top and bottom (**Figure 1**).

5   Place the pillow front atop the backing with right sides facing. Stitch around the outer edge of the pillow top, rounding the corners if you prefer to avoid sharp points on the finished pillow (**Figure 2**).

TIP: *Sew around the entire pillow twice for additional strength.*

6   Turn the pillow right side out through the opening in the pillow back. Gently push out the corners of the pillow with a point turner and insert the pillow form.

Hexagon Pillow by Linda Hungerford.

ENVELOPE BACK WITH BINDING

1 Cut the fabric the height of the finished pillow (without an additional seam allowance) and the width of the finished pillow plus 6" (15 cm) (for overlap). As an example, for a 16" (40.5 cm) pillow, cut (2) 22" × 16½" (56 cm × 42 cm) rectangles.

2 Follow steps 1–4 for the Envelope Back Without Binding.

3 Place the pillow front on the backing, wrong sides together. Machine baste around the pillow layers, ⅛" (3 cm) from the outer edge.

4 From the binding fabric, cut enough 2¼" (5.5 cm) strips to go around the perimeter of the pillow, plus an extra 5" (12.5 cm). Using diagonal seams, join binding strips into one continuous piece for straight-grain, French-fold binding (see French-Fold Binding in this chapter for tips). Bind the pillow as you would a quilt and insert the pillow form.

French-Fold Binding
(AKA DOUBLE-FOLD BINDING)

A well-made binding will protect the edges of your quilt, add to the overall design, and make it last longer. The following technique is for creating a French-fold binding, also known as a double-fold binding.

PREPARE THE BINDING

1   Measure the perimeter of your quilt and then add approximately 24" (61 cm). The additional length will accommodate the mitered corners and the finished ends of the binding, and give you a few inches to spare.

2   Cut enough 2¼"-wide (5.5 cm) strips to equal the desired length.

3   Join the strips together using diagonal seams. To do this, place two strips, right sides together at right angles. The area where the strips overlap forms a square. Sew diagonally across the square (**Figure 1**). Trim the excess fabric ¼" (6 mm) from the seam line and press the seam allowance open.

4   Lightly press the binding in half lengthwise, with wrong sides facing.

ATTACH THE BINDING

5   Open up the binding and press ½" (1.3 cm) to the wrong side at one short end. Refold the binding lengthwise. Choose a starting point along one side of the quilt, at least 8" (20.5 cm) from the corner. Leaving several inches of the folded end of the binding loose at the beginning, align the raw edges of the binding strip to the raw edges of the right side of the quilt top. Pin or clip in place. Begin sewing, using a ¼" (6 mm) seam allowance.

6   Stop sewing ¼" (6 mm) before reaching the corner, backstitch, clip the threads, and remove the quilt from the sewing machine.

7   Rotate the quilt 90-degree to position it for sewing the next side. Fold the binding fabric up away from the project (**Figure 2**). Then, fold the binding back down along the project raw edge. This forms a miter at the corner. Stitch the second side beginning at the raw edge and continuing down the second side, ending ¼" (6 mm) from the next corner (**Figure 3**). Continue to add the binding to the remainder of the quilt.

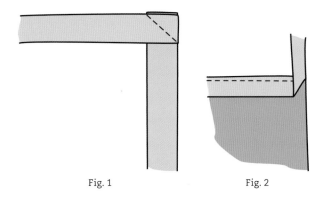

Fig. 1   Fig. 2

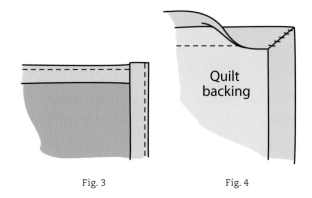

Fig. 3   Fig. 4

8 To finish the binding, stop stitching several inches from the starting point. Measure and trim the working edge to fit at least ½" (1.3 cm) under the folded edge of the beginning end of the binding. Trim the binding at that point.

9 Slide the trimmed end under the folded edge and finish sewing the binding.

10 Fold the binding to the back of the quilt, enclosing the raw edges. The folded edge of the binding strip should just cover the stitches visible on the back of the quilt (**Figure 4**).

11 Sew the binding in place by hand, tucking in the corners to complete the miters as you go. Slipstitch the folds for a tidy finish.

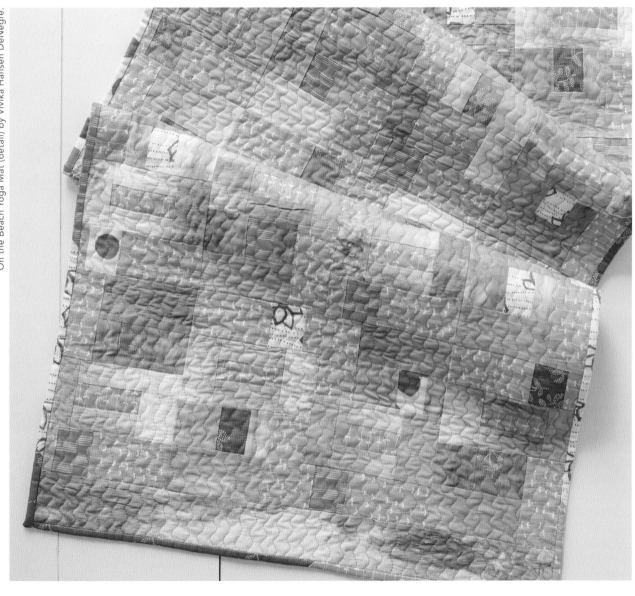

On the Beach Yoga Mat (detail) by Vivika Hansen DeNegre.

2

HOME DÉCOR & ACCESSORIES

FROM THE LIVING ROOM TO THE KITCHEN. CREATIVE DESIGNS TO HELP FEATHER YOUR NEST

Refer to chapter 1: Quilting Basics for instructions on a variety of the quilting techniques found in this book.

FINISHED SIZE

17" (43 cm) square

MATERIALS

Background fabric, 18" (45.5 cm) square (natural linen used here)

Hexies for pillow top, (19) 2½" (6.5 cm) squares (18 print, 1 white)

Muslin, 18" (45.5 cm) square

Backing, ½ yard (0.5 m)

Binding, ¼ yard (0.2 m)

Low-loft cotton batting, 18" (45.5 cm) square

Pillow insert, 16" (40.5 cm)

Thread, 50wt, pale gray

Straw needle, #10

Embroidery needle, #7 for quilting

Perle cotton, size 8 (in colors to complement the hexagon prints used here)

Clover Wonder Clips

Hera marker (optional)

Small ruler

Embroidery hoop, 12" (30.5 cm)

Thread conditioner, such as Thread Heaven

1" (2.5 cm) hexagon papers, template provided in templates section or use 19 precut papers

All seams are ¼" (6 mm) unless otherwise noted.

HEXAGON PILLOW

LINDA HUNGERFORD

Illustrations by Sue Friend

Quilters who find themselves away from home—and their sewing machines—will find this hand-stitched pillow the perfect project during long car rides, while waiting to pick up kids, or passing time on the deck of a cruise ship. Three different hand techniques are used: English paper piecing, appliqué, and big stitch quilting. Once you're back home, use your sewing machine to turn the top into a pillow.

PLUMP THAT PILLOW

When choosing a pillow form, select one a size larger than the pillow cover. Your pillow will appear plumper—and the pillow corners will be stuffed.

MAKE THE HEXAGONS

If you plan to wash the finished pillow, prewash and press the fabrics before cutting (see Basting the Hexagons sidebar for tips.)

1 Place a 1" (2.5 cm) paper hexagon on the wrong side of a 2½" (6.5 cm) fabric square. Fold the fabric over each edge of the hexagon, using a clip to hold it in place.

2 Baste the fabric squares around the hexagon papers, using your favorite method. Baste all 19 hexagons (**Figure 1**).

Basting the Hexagons

As with many quilting techniques, there is no single, do-it-this-way-or-else method to baste the fabric around the paper hexagons. The best way is to use the method you enjoy the most—and provides you with consistent results.

Here are some tried-and-true methods:

- Use a small dot of basting glue to attach the fabric to the hexagon paper.

- Thread baste through the fabric and the paper. This is recommended if the papers are more than 1" (2.5 cm) long on any side.

- Thread baste on the corners of the fabric only. With this method, basting stitches can be left in when the papers are removed from the back.

Thread Basting How-To

Because this project uses small hexagon papers, thread basting the corners of the fabric is a good option. To do so, thread a straw needle with gray thread. After knotting 1 end, take a small stitch through the fabric at 1 corner, and then make a backstitch there to secure. Move to the next corner, take another small stitch and a backstitch. Continue folding and stitching at each corner until the hexagon is completely basted, then clip the thread.

ARRANGE THE HEXAGONS

3 Arrange the basted hexagons for the pillow top.

NOTE: *Hexies are fun to rearrange. Try your own design or refer to Figure 3 for placement!*

JOIN THE HEXAGONS

4 Place the center (white) hexagon and an outer hexagon right sides together, aligning 1 edge.

5 Use a straw needle and gray thread to stitch just the very edges of the fold together. Use short whip stitches or ladder stitches, ⅟₁₆" (2 mm) apart (**Figure 2**).

6 Continue adding hexagons until the unit is complete. As needed, secure stitching with a knot on the paper side of the hexagons. Take an extra stitch at each Y-seam, the corner where 3 hexagons join (see Sew Perfect Y-Seams in chapter 1 for tips).

7 Join all 19 hexagons.

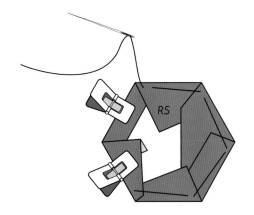

Fig. 1

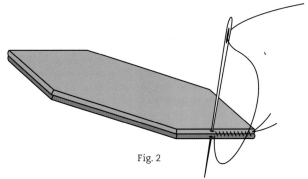

Fig. 2

APPLIQUÉ THE HEXAGON UNIT

8 Fold the 18" (45.5 cm) linen fabric in quarters and pin mark the center.

9 Align the center of the hexagon unit with the pin mark.

NOTE: *The hexagon papers have not been removed.*

10 Pin or hand baste the hexagon unit to the linen fabric.

11 Use a straw needle with gray thread to appliqué the hexagon unit to the linen fabric.

TIP: *The pillow here was made with a 50wt pale gray thread as it blends with both the hexagon prints and the linen background.*

12 With the wrong side of the pillow top facing up, carefully cut away the background fabric ¼" (6 mm) from the appliqué stitches (**Figure 3**).

NOTE: *Using small embroidery scissors with sharp tips will make this much easier.*

13 Remove all hexagon papers.

NOTE: *If you have basted through the paper, snip and remove the basting threads.*

14 To remove bulk and prevent fabric shadowing on the pillow top, trim excess fabric from each hexagon, leaving ¼" (6 mm) seam allowance.

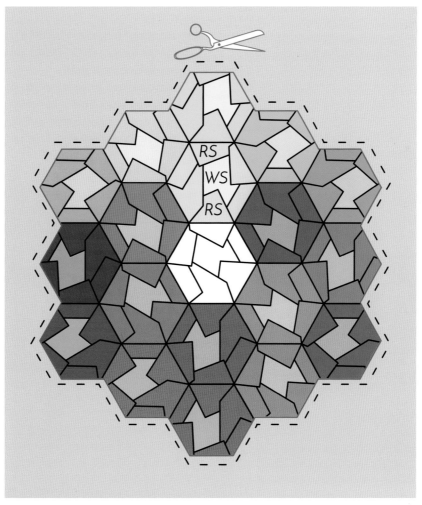

Fig. 3

QUILT THE PILLOW

15 Layer the appliquéd pillow top, batting, and muslin to make a quilt sandwich. Baste.

16 Thread the embroidery needle with perle cotton. Beginning at the center of the hexagon appliqué, quilt a running stitch through all layers ¼" (6 mm) from the edge of each hexagon. Stitches should be approximately ⅛" (3 mm) apart (**Figure 4**).

NOTE: *Use an embroidery hoop, if desired.*

17 Following **Figure 5** and after quilting the first hexagon round, use a ruler and Hera marker to mark quilting lines on the linen background which echo the outline. Mark the first quilting line (red) ¼" (6 mm) from the hexagon edge. Subsequent quilting lines are ½" (1.3 cm) from the first quilting line (orange), ¾" (2 cm) from the second quilting line (yellow), 1¼" (3.2 cm) from the third quilting line (green), and 1½" (3.8 cm) from the fourth quilting line (aqua).

18 With the appliqué centered, trim the pillow top to 15½" (39.5 cm).

SEW THE PILLOW

19 Cut 2 pieces from the backing fabric, each 12½" × 15½" (31.5 cm × 39.5 cm).

20 Hem 1 of the backing pieces along the 15½" (39.5 cm) edge by pressing ½" (1.3 cm) to the wrong side. Press another ½" (1.3 cm) under. Edgestitch along the first fold. Repeat on the other backing piece.

21 With the wrong side of backing pieces face up and the sewn edges in the center, position the backing pieces to 15½" (39.5 cm) square. Pin the overlapped raw edges. (See Easy Envelope Pillow Backs in chapter 1 for more tips.)

22 Clip or pin the pillow top to the backing, wrong sides together.

OPTIONAL: *Machine baste the pieces together, ¼" (6 mm) from each raw edge.*

23 To make French-fold binding, cut 2 binding strips 2¼" (5.5 cm) × WOF (width-of-fabric). Sew the binding strips together with a diagonal seam, trimming and pressing these seams open, creating one long strip. Fold and press the binding strip in half, wrong sides together. Bind as desired. (See French-Fold Binding in chapter 1 for directions.)

24 Insert the pillow form.

Photo by Linda Hungerford

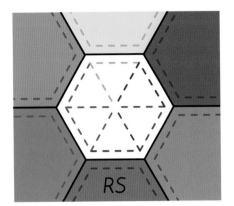

Fig. 4

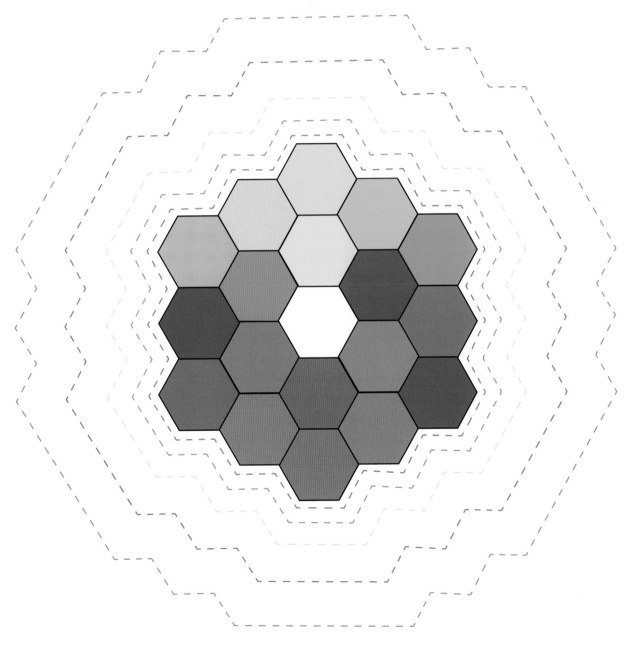

Fig. 5

FINISHED SIZE

4½" × 12" (11.5 cm × 30.5 cm)

MATERIALS

Background fabric, ¼ yard (0.2 m)
gray (paper pieces 3, 4, and 5)

Off-white fabric, ⅛ yard (0.1 m)
for pencil "wood" (paper piece 1)

Scraps, (8) 2½" × 3½"
(6.5 cm × 9 cm) strips for pencil
shafts (paper piece 6)

Scraps, (8) 1" (2.5 cm) squares for
pencil points (paper piece 2)

Lightweight woven fusible
interfacing, ¼ yard (0.2 m)

Container, 5¼" tall × 12"
(13.5 cm × 30.5 cm) circumference

Pencil Holder paper-piecing
templates (see Templates section)

*All seams are ¼" (6 mm) unless
otherwise noted.*

PENCIL HOLDER

GOSIA PAWLOWSKA

Designer Gosia Pawlowska loves small, fun
projects, so she created this modern pencil
holder suitable for any studio or office. Many of
the pieces are quite small so this paper-pieced
project is great for making use of colorful scraps.

USE YOUR STASH

Pair large and small colorful scraps to
create pencil points and shafts of the
pencil.

CUTTING INSTRUCTIONS

Make 8 copies of the paper-piecing pattern. Directions and cutting instructions create the project as pictured. See the Customize This Project sidebar to create a smaller or larger cover. Press seams open whenever possible.

FROM BACKGROUND FABRIC, CUT:

(1) 5" × 12½" (12.5 cm × 31.5 cm) rectangle for lining

(8) 2" × 2½" (5 cm × 6.5 cm) rectangles for paper piece 5

(8) 2" (5 cm) squares; cut each square in half diagonally to create 16 triangles for paper pieces 3 and 4

FROM OFF-WHITE FABRIC, CUT:

(8) 1¾" × 2½" (4.5 cm × 6.5 cm) rectangles for paper piece 1

FROM INTERFACING, CUT:

(1) 4½" × 12" (11.5 cm × 30.5 cm) rectangle

MAKE THE PENCIL HOLDER COVER

1 Referring to the Foundation Paper-Piecing directions in chapter 1, paper piece 8 "pencils" following the numbering of the pieces on the pattern.

2 Using **Figure 1** as a guide, arrange the pencils in a row. Sew the pencils together, matching the seams, to create a panel.

3 Press the interfacing to the reverse side of the panel, centering the interfacing and leaving the seam allowances free.

4 Right sides together, sew the panel to the lining along the 2 long seams only.

5 Turn the cover right side out and press the seams.

6 Topstitch along both seams.

7 Fold the cover in half, right sides together, and sew the short seam. Press open.

8 Turn the cover right side out and slide onto the container.

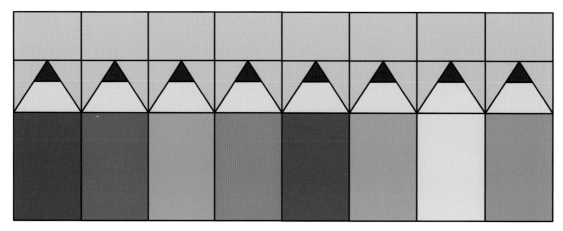

Fig. 1

Customize This Project

This versatile cover can be customized to fit almost any size container by making the following adjustments. When changing the size, adjust the fabric requirements as necessary.

> **TIP**: *Choose and measure the container before sewing.*

- To accommodate a wider or narrower container, add or subtract a "pencil." Each pencil finishes at 1½" (3.8 cm) wide.

- To accommodate a taller or shorter container, adjust paper piece 5 (above the pencil point) and/or paper piece 6 (the pencil shaft) on the paper-piecing pattern.

- For any size, the cover will fit best on a container with straight sides.

- Make colored pencils—with colorful points that match the pencil shafts like in Gosia's project—or make all the points graphite gray like in the Cover Assembly Diagram.

- You can also create your own designs, using miniature Quilt blocks, for example, as shown here.

Photo by Gosia Pawlowska

FINISHED SIZE

14" × 40" (35.5 × 101.5 cm)

MATERIALS

Background fabric, 1¼ yards
(1.1 m)

Braid fabric, 15 fat quarters
(18" × 22" [45.5 cm × 56 cm]) or
assorted scraps for (100) 1¼" × 5"
(3.2 cm × 12.5 cm) rectangles and
(1) 3" (7.5 cm) square

Backing, ½ yard (0.5 m)

Binding, ¼ yard (0.2 m)

Batting, 18" × 50"
(45.5 cm × 127 cm) rectangles

*All seams are ¼" (6 mm) unless
otherwise noted.*

BRAIDED TABLE RUNNER

DAISY ASCHEHOUG

Illustrations by Daisy Aschehoug

Although it may look complex, this stunning table runner uses a simple, Log Cabin-style construction method. The resulting design is a colorful centerpiece that will dress up any table or occassion.

CUTTING INSTRUCTIONS

FROM FAT QUARTERS (OR SCRAPS), CUT:

(100) 1½" × 5" (3.8 cm × 12.5 cm) rectangles

MAKE THE BRAID

1   Cut the 3" (7.5 cm) square in half along the diagonal (**Figure 1**).

2   With right sides together, align one of the rectangles along the edge of the triangle. Sew along the long edge (**Figure 2**).

3   Press the strip back (**Figure 3**).

4   Sew the next strip to the opposite side (**Figure 4**). Press the strip back (**Figure 5**).

6   Continuing sewing strips to the opposite sides, until the braid reaches 45" (114.5 cm).

7   Trim the braid to 5" × 40" (12.5 cm × 101.5 cm) (**Figure 6**).

COMPLETE THE TOP

8   Trim the selvedges from the background fabric. Cut (2) 5" × 40" (12.5 cm × 101.5 cm) pieces for the side panels, parallel to the selvedge. Cut (1) 18" × 45" (45.5 cm × 114.5 cm) piece for the backing, also parallel to the selvedge.

9   Sew side panels to either side of the braid (**Figure 7**).

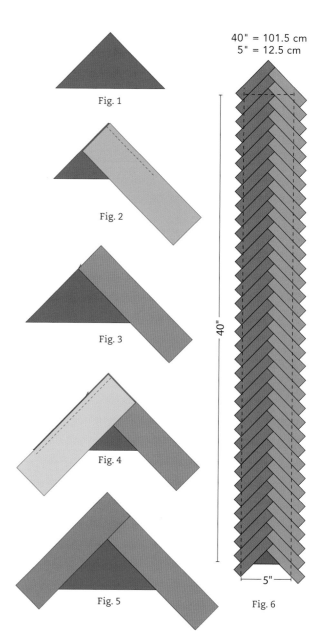

40" = 101.5 cm
5" = 12.5 cm

Fig. 1

Fig. 2

Fig. 3

Fig. 4

Fig. 5

Fig. 6

40"

5"

FINISH THE TABLE RUNNER

10 Make the quilt sandwich by placing the backing wrong side up, followed by the batting, and then the quilt top, right side up. Baste.

11 Quilt as desired. The featured runner was made with a 3.3 mm stitch length and quilted straight lines in the background along the length of the runner.

12 Cut binding fabric into 2¼" (5.5 cm) strips. Sew 4 strips together with diagonal seams to create a single binding strip. Fold the strip in half lengthwise and press. Bind the quilt as desired. (See French-Fold Binding in chapter 1 for directions.)

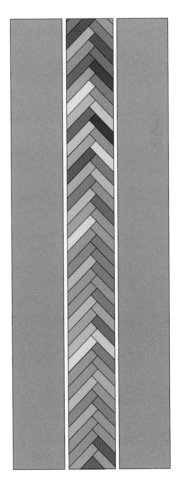

Fig. 7

FINISHED SIZE

9½" × 24½" (24 cm × 62 cm)

FINISHED BLOCK SIZE

3½" (9 cm) square

MATERIALS

Fabric scraps, (24) at least 4" (10 cm) square each

Background fabric, 1¼ yard (1.1 m)

Pocket backing fabric, 11" × 27" (28 cm × 68.5 cm) (not visible)

Print fabric, (2) 4½" (11.4 cm) × WOF (width-of-fabric) strips for the underside of ties

Batting, 11" × 27" (28 cm × 68.5 cm) rectangle

Walking foot for straight-line quilting

3½" (9 cm) quarter circle templates A and B (see Templates section)

OPTIONAL

Spray starch

Square ruler, 3½" (9 cm) square

Template plastic or cardboard

Rotary cutting supplies

All seams are ¼" (6 mm) unless otherwise noted.

This charming apron was inspired by a challenge to the Modern Quilt Guild staff members at the first-ever QuiltCon. One of the necessities of working the show was an apron, and to make hers, Jen turned to her background in quilting. She loves quarter circles and their gentle curves so she made a mini quilt and turned it into a generous pocket extending along the whole front of the apron. Play with color and quilting designs to make this project in your own signature style.

CUTTING DIRECTIONS

Trace the quarter circle templates A and B onto template plastic or cardboard. Cut out the templates carefully so the pieces fit together accurately.

FROM BACKGROUND FABRIC, CUT:

(2) 2½" (6.5 cm) × WOF (width-of-fabric) strips for the binding

(2) 4½" (11.5 cm) × WOF strips for the ties

(1) 15" × 25" (38 cm × 63.5 cm) rectangle for the apron body

(1) 5" × 26" (12.5 cm × 66 cm) rectangle for the waistband

(2) 4" (10 cm) × WOF strips for the concave pieces (template B)

24 concave pieces using template B

FROM SCRAP FABRIC, CUT:

24 quarter circles using template A

SEWING CURVES

1   Fold a convex quarter circle (template A) in half and lightly pinch the fold to mark the center. Fold and pinch the concave piece and mark the center of the curve. Match the pieces with right sides together, aligning the centers of each piece and pin in place (**Figure 1**).

2   Pin the outside edges of each piece together, ensuring the straight edges match (**Figure 2**). Add more pins until the 2 pieces are pinned together and the concave curve is flat against the convex quarter circle (**Figure 3**).

NOTE: *Everyone sews curves differently—using pins, no pins, or a special foot on the sewing machine. I prefer to use pins because it helps me achieve a perfect curve. Do what works best for you!*

3   Using a scant ¼" (6 mm) seam allowance, sew the curve. Sew slowly until you get the hang of it.

4   Press the seams toward the center. Using a bit of spray starch or fabric stabilizer is very useful in helping the curve lay flat. Make 24 quarter circle units.

5   Trim the blocks to 3½" (9 cm) square. Using a 3½" (9 cm) square ruler will help you do this quickly and accurately.

TIP: *Batching tasks helps to establish a more efficient routine when sewing. This means to pin all the pieces, sew them all, press them all, and finally square them all up.*

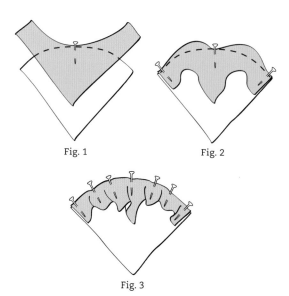

Fig. 1   Fig. 2

Fig. 3

Straight-Line Quilting Tips

Here are a few tips to help you get the perfect stitch.

- Use a walking foot.

- Lengthen your stitch length by at least 1. I piece at 2.0 and straight-line quilt at 3.0 and sometimes even 3.5.

- Practice.

- Reduce the pressure on the presser foot.

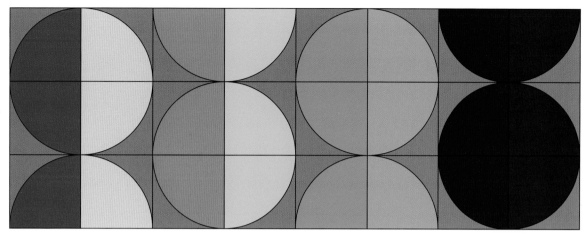

Fig. 4

ASSEMBLE THE APRON

6   Referring to **Figure 4**, arrange the blocks for the pocket as shown and sew them together, matching the seams.

7   Create a quilt sandwich by layering the pocket backing fabric wrong side up, followed by the batting, and then the pieced pocket top, right side up. Baste with pins.

8   Quilt as desired. The apron pocket shown here was quilted with straight lines in a diamond pattern.

9   Once the quilting is complete, trim the edges of the quilted pocket.

10   Sew the binding strips together to create 1 piece of binding. Bind the top edge of the pocket using your preferred method, and trim the edges flush. Place the quilted pocket on top of the apron body fabric, aligning the bottom of the pocket with the bottom of the apron fabric. Match the raw edges. If the pieces do not match exactly, trim them to size. This may happen if the quilting is very dense, as the pocket will shrink a bit.

11   Baste the pocket to the apron fabric using a scant ¼" (6 mm) seam.

12   Make the pocket dividers by sewing a straight line (see Straight-Line Quilting Tips sidebar) from the top of the pocket to the bottom. In this apron there are 2 small pockets and 1 large. The sewing begins on the seam lines between the pink/orange

and the yellow/green blocks. Since this is a stress point of the apron, backstitch at the top of the pocket a few times for security.

13   Use the remaining binding to bind the sides and bottom of the apron.

14   Fold in the ends of the waistband fabric by approximately ½" (1.3 cm) and press. Fold the whole piece of fabric in half lengthwise, matching the raw edges and press. Open it up, then press 1 long edge up ¼" (6 mm).

15   Place the waistband on top of the main fabric and line up the raw edges. (The side you pressed up ¼" [6 mm] will be facing you). Adjust the length of the waistband as needed to ensure the edges line up and sew. Press the seam toward the waistband.

16   Fold the waistband over to encase the seam allowance and topstitch.

17   Layer a print tie fabric with a background tie fabric, right sides together. At 1 end, cut an angle to give the end of the tie a point. Sew along the long sides and the angled end. Turn the tie right side out, press, and topstitch around the perimeter. Repeat for the second tie.

18   Create a small pleat at the raw end of the ties. Insert the tie into the waistband, pin, and then topstitch.

FINISHED SIZE

15½" (39.5 cm) square

MATERIALS

Assorted fabric scraps, 6 strips approximately 1" × 5" (2.5 cm × 12.5 cm) each

NOTE: *These are the starter strips for the foundation-pieced petals.*

Assorted fabric selvedges, approximately 4–6" (10–15 cm) each

NOTE: *You will need 4–8 selvedge strips for each petal, depending on the width of each selvedge.*

Background fabric, 16½" (42 cm) square

Lining fabric, 16½" (42 cm) square

Scrap fabric for the selvedge foundation, (6) 5" (12.5 cm) squares

Flower center, 5" (12.5 cm) square

Pillow back fabric, (2) 11½" × 16" (29 cm × 40.5 cm) rectangles

Lightweight fusible web, ⅜ yard (0.3 m)

Narrow rickrack for stem, 6" (15 cm) strip

Batting, 16½" (42 cm) square

Button

Pillow form, 16" (40.5 cm) square

Temporary spray adhesive

Template plastic or cardboard

Hexagon pattern (see Templates section)

All seams are ¼" (6 mm) unless otherwise noted.

BLOOM SELVEDGE PILLOW

CINDY WIENS

Selvedge edges, the part of the fabric we usually cut off before starting a quilting project, have a lot of fun information. They often include the names of the designer, the fabric collection, and the manufacturer, as well as the colored registration dots that indicate the colors used during printing. This pillow is an easy project that showcases the selvedge information, repurposing something you'd normally toss into a charming record of your fabric stash.

MAKE THE FLOWER

1 To make each petal, position (1) 1" × 5"
(2.5 cm × 12.5 cm) scrap fabric strip even with
the lower edge of the 5" (12.5 cm) foundation
fabric square. Place a selvedge strip on top of
this scrap fabric, ½–¾" (1.3–2 cm) from the lower
edge, so the finished edge of the selvedge is
toward the bottom. Sew the selvedge strip in
place, topstitching close to the finished edge
(**Figure 1**).

2 Position the next selvedge strip on the foundation
fabric with the lower edge overlapping the upper
raw edge of the first strip. Sew the second strip in
place close to the finished edge. Continue sewing selvedge strips in place until the foundation is
covered (**Figure 2**).

3 Trace the hexagon pattern onto template plastic
or cardboard; cut out. Using the template, trace 7
hexagons onto the paper side of the fusible web.
Cut each piece out about ⅛" (3 mm) from the
drawn line. Fuse the hexagons to the wrong side
of each selvedge foundation unit and the flower
center fabric. Cut on the traced line and peel away
the paper backing (**Figure 3**).

4 Place the petals and flower center on the 16½"
(42 cm) background square. Start with the top
center petal and place it about 1½" (3.8 cm)
down from the raw edge. After placing the center
bottom petal in place, insert the rickrack stem just
underneath the bottom raw edge.

5 Following the manufacturer's instructions, fuse the
center and the petals in place. Machine appliqué
each fused piece into place using a small zigzag
stitch, wide enough to catch both sides of the
petals and the center wherever they touch. Stitch
the rickrack in place.

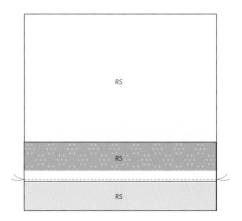

Fig. 1

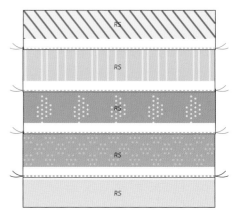

Fig. 2

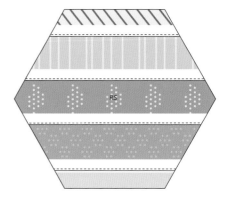

Fig. 3

FINISH THE PILLOW

6 Layer the batting between the lining fabric and the pillow top. Use temporary spray adhesive to baste the layers together.

7 Quilt the pillow cover as desired. For the pillow shown here, the selvedge petals were used as a guideline to echo the quilt ¼" (6 mm) from the hexagons with brightly colored thread.

8 Trim away the excess backing and batting, and square up the pillow top to 16" (40.5 cm) square.

9 Place 1 backing piece wrong side up. Fold one 16" (40.5 cm) edge ¼" (6 mm) to the wrong side and press; repeat. Sew the folded edge in place. This backing piece now measures 11" × 16" (28 cm × 40.5 cm) and has 1 finished edge. Repeat with the other backing piece.

10 Place the pillow top right side up. Position 1 backing piece right side down with the finished edge toward the center line. Place the other backing piece on top of the first with its finished edge also toward the center. The backing pieces will overlap in the center, allowing for insertion of the pillow form. Pin the backing pieces in place and machine stitch ¼" (6 mm) from the perimeter, all the way around. (See Easy Envelope Pillow Backs in chapter 1 for tips.)

11 Turn the pillow cover right side out and insert the pillow form.

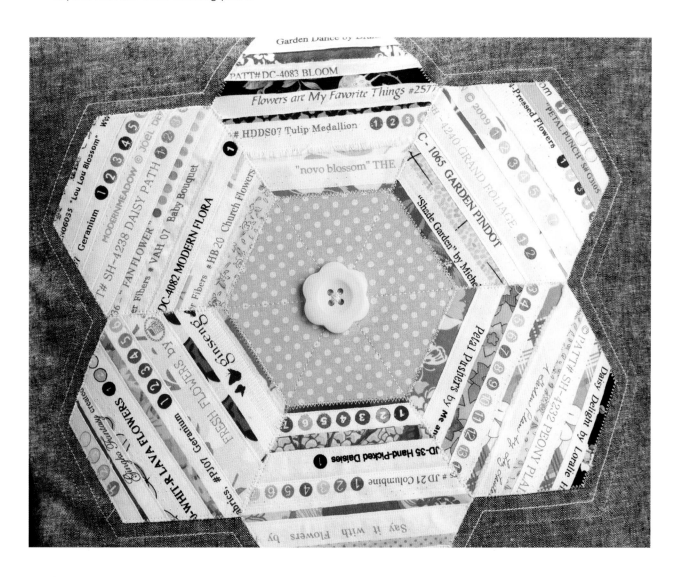

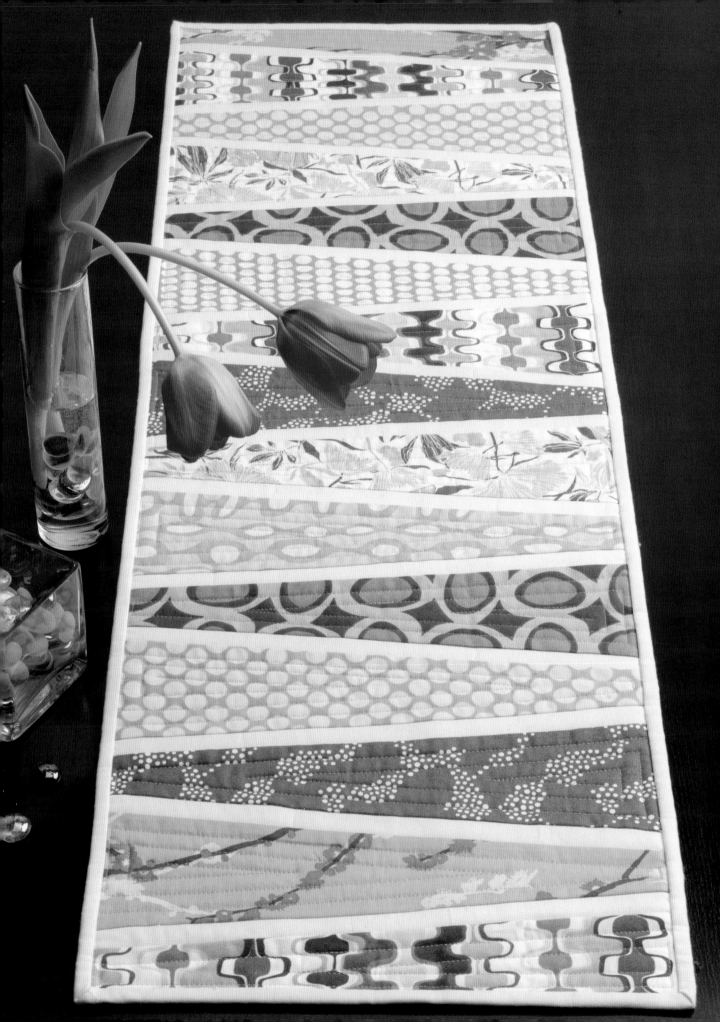

FINISHED SIZE

13" × 40½" (33 cm × 103 cm)

MATERIALS

15 assorted gray and yellow prints, (1) 4" × 14" (10 cm × 35.5 cm) rectangle from each

Solid yellow fabric for divider strips and binding, ½ yard (0.5 m)

Backing fabric, ¾ yard (0.7 m)

Low-loft cotton batting, 18" × 46" (45.5 cm × 117 cm) piece

Basting safety pins

Tape

Rotary cutting supplies

Template plastic or cardboard

Wedge pattern (see Templates section)

All seams are ¼ " (6 mm) unless otherwise noted.

REFLECTED WEDGES RUNNER

JACQUIE GERING

Traditional Dresden Plate wedges come together in a new way to create a delightfully modern feeling table runner. Echo quilting in the wedges completes the polished feel.

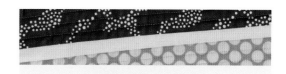

ADJUSTING THE SIZE OF YOUR RUNNER

This runner can be easily customized for the size of your table. Make it wider by using a longer wedge template, or shorten or lengthen it by subtracting or adding wedges.

CUTTING DIRECTIONS

Trace the wedge pattern onto template plastic or cardboard and cut out. Be sure to trace and cut accurately.

FROM THE 15 PRINT RECTANGLES, CUT:

15 wedges using the wedge template

FROM THE SOLID YELLOW FABRIC, CUT:

(7) 1" (2.5 cm) × WOF (width-of-fabric) strips; subcut into (14) 1" × 16" (2.5 cm × 40.5 cm) strips.

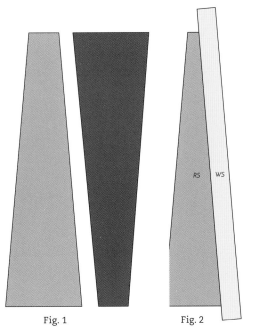

Fig. 1   Fig. 2

ARRANGE THE WEDGES

1   Arrange the 15 wedges in a row, alternating the short and long ends of the wedges (**Figure 1**).

   TIP: *Placing different values next to each other will create more interest and movement in your table runner.*

2   When you are satisfied with the arrangement of the prints, pin a yellow strip, right sides together, to the right side of each wedge (**Figure 2**).

   NOTE: *The strip will extend beyond the edges of the wedge.*

3   Sew, and press the seam toward the wedge. Do this for all of the wedges except for the final wedge in the row.

4   Place the wedges back in order.

5   Sew the wedges together in order from left to right to create a panel, placing right sides together and matching the raw edges. To help line up the wedges for sewing, place 2 wedges side by side. Place a pin where the right corner of the first wedge meets the left corner of the second wedge as shown in **Figure 3**.

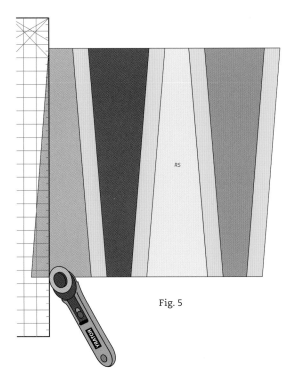

Fig. 5

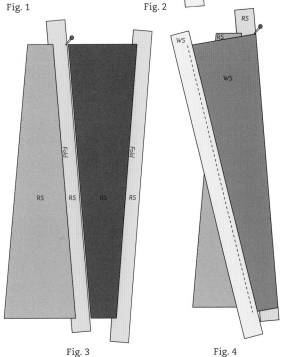

Fig. 3   Fig. 4

6 Place the second wedge right side down on the first wedge, aligning the corner of the wedge with the pin (**Figure 4**). Sew, and press the seam toward the wedge.

7 Repeat to create a panel of wedges.

8 Place the panel of wedges on your cutting mat and trim the panel to 13" (33 cm) wide, making sure the top and bottom edges of the panel are parallel.

9 Align the top of the panel with a horizontal line on the cutting mat. Trim the ends of the panel so that they are perpendicular to the top and bottom of the panel (**Figure 5**).

FINISH THE TABLE RUNNER

10 From the backing fabric, cut (1) 17" × 40" (43 cm × 101.5 cm) strip and (1) 6½" × 17" (16.5 cm × 43 cm) strip. Sew the 2 strips together along the 17" (43 cm) side. Press the seam to the side to finish the backing.

11 Press the backing and place it wrong side up on a flat surface. Tape the 4 sides of the backing to the flat surface, making sure it is taut but not stretched. Center the batting on top of the backing, making sure there are no wrinkles. Then place the table runner top right side up on the batting, centering it.

12 Baste the quilt sandwich with safety pins.

13 Machine or hand quilt the layers together as desired, removing the safety pins as you quilt. The featured table runner is machine quilted with echo quilting within each wedge.

14 Trim the batting and backing even with the top to prepare it for binding. From the solid yellow fabric, cut (3) 2¼" (5.5 cm) × WOF strips. Join the binding strips. (See French-Fold Binding in chapter 1 for directions.)

FINISHED SIZE

4" × 9" × 12" (10 cm × 23 cm × 30.5 cm)

MATERIALS

Linen, ⅝ yard (0.6 m)

Accent fabric, ¼ yard (0.2 m)

Flower fabric, ⅛ yard (0.1 m)

Lining, ⅜ yard (0.3 m)

Fusible interfacing, ½ yard (0.5 m)

Water-soluble marker

Jar lid, about 3" (7.5 cm) in diameter

All seams are ¼" (6 mm) unless otherwise indicated.

TWISTED FLOWER TOTE

VANESSA CHRISTENSON

Illustrations by Sue Friend

Vanessa has always loved working with linen. For this project she paired linen with beautiful pink prints from her Simply Color Collection for Moda. The linen gives the bag body without adding stiffness, and the cotton fabrics work well for the twisted flower and other accents. Any girl, little or big, will love this tote!

CUTTING DIRECTIONS

FROM THE LINEN FABRIC, CUT:

(2) 6½" × 12½" (16.5 cm × 31.5 cm) rectangles for the outer tote

(2) 18" × 5" (45.5 cm × 12.5 cm) strips for the straps

FROM THE ACCENT FABRIC, CUT:

(2) 5½" × 12½" (14 cm × 31.5 cm) rectangles for the outer tote accent

FROM THE FLOWER FABRIC, CUT:

(2) 1½" (3.8 cm) × WOF (width-of-fabric) strips for the twisted flower embellishment

FROM THE LINING FABRIC, CUT:

(1) 12½" × 22½" (31.5 cm × 57 cm) rectangle for the lining

(2) 11½" × 9½" (29 cm × 24 cm) rectangles for the lining pockets

START THE BAG

1. With right sides together, sew (1) 6½" × 12½" (16.5 cm × 31.5 cm) linen rectangle and (1) 5½" × 12½" (14 cm × 31.5 cm) accent fabric rectangle together along the 12½" (31.5 cm) edge. Press toward the accent fabric. Make 2.

2. Topstitch the seam using matching thread.

3. Cut (2) 11½" × 12½" (29 cm × 31.5 cm) pieces of fusible interfacing and fuse to the wrong sides of the outer tote pieces.

MAKE THE FLOWER

4. Sew the 2 pieces of flower fabric together at one short end to create 1 long strip.

5. On 1 linen/accent fabric piece, measure ¾" (2 cm) from the top edge and 2" (5 cm) from the right side. Place the outer edge of the jar lid there and trace it with the water-soluble marker. This is the placement guide for the twisted flower.

6. Fold 1 end of the strip lengthwise, wrong sides together and fold it again. Do not press the strip. Pinch the end and place it on the drawn circle, securing only the end with a pin.

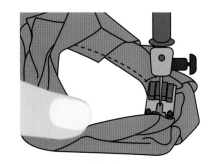

Fig. 1

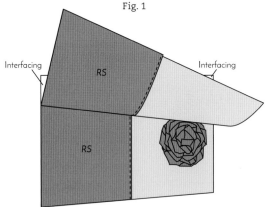

Fig. 2

TIP: *You will stop and start frequently as you sew the flower. Always end with your needle down to hold the fabric in place as you refold and twist it.*

7. Sew a few stitches into your folded edge and backstitch to secure. Gently twist the strip outward and refold as needed. Sew the twisted strip to the drawn circle on the inner edge of the twist (about ⅛–¼" [3–6 mm] from the inside edge). Continue gently twisting and sewing around the entire drawn circle, covering over the beginning of the strip and completing the full circle (**Figure 1**).

TIP: *Fold and twist the strip just a few inches at a time, sew it down, then stop to refold and twist.*

8. Continue sewing the folded and twisted strip, working inward, overlapping the inside edges of the previous circle to prevent gaps. If the strip ends before you finish the flower, start another strip, backstitching to secure the end. End the circle in the center by folding the raw edge under and backstitching.

NOTE: *This embellishment is fun and not meant to be perfect! Some of the wrong side of the fabric or a bit of the tote may show through. That is OK.*

9 With right sides together, pin the 2 outer tote pieces together along the bottom edge and sew to create a 12½" × 22½" (31.5 cm × 57 cm) panel (**Figure 2**). Set aside.

MAKE THE STRAPS

10 Fold the 18" × 5" (45.5 cm × 12.5 cm) linen strips in half lengthwise, wrong sides together, and press. Open the strip and turn the raw edges in to meet the pressed crease. Press. Refold the strip, encasing the raw edges. Edgestitch the outer edges of both straps. Set aside.

11 With the outer tote facing right side up, pin 1 strap to the linen 3" (7.5 cm) in from the side. The raw edges of the strap should overhang the edge ¼" (6 mm). Repeat with the other strap on the opposite side.

CREATE THE LINING

12 To make a pocket, fold the 11½" × 9½" (29 cm × 24 cm) rectangles in half with right sides together. Sew around the 3 open edges leaving a 3" (7.5 cm) opening on 1 side of your folded fabric. Turn the pocket right side out. Press. Topstitch the folded edge. (This will be the top of the pocket.)

TIP: *Fold in half and finger press the middle of the length of the pocket to mark where you are going to sew the pocket to subdivide it into 2 small pockets.*

13 Fold the lining fabric in half horizontally with wrong sides together and finger press a crease to mark the middle of your length.

14 From the folded edge measure 3" (7.5 cm) up and make a mark with a water-soluble marker or place a pin. Repeat on the other side of the crease.

15 Fold the lining in half vertically to find the center.

16 Using the crease as your guide and the marked 3" (7.5 cm) line, pin the pocket in place. Topstitch both sides and the bottom of the pocket. Sew vertically on the pocket to create 2 small pockets.

ASSEMBLE AND FINISH THE BAG

17 On a flat surface place the outside panel right side up with the straps pinned in place. Place the lining right side down on the panel. Sew the 12½" (31.5 cm) sides, be sure to remove the pins keeping the straps in place. This will create a huge fabric loop.

18 With right sides still together, reposition the sewn "loop" of fabric so the seams match up. This will place the lining on 1 side and the outer bag on the other side.

19 Pin down the long open edges on both sides. Stitch, leaving a 3–4" (7.5–10 cm) opening on 1 side of the lining.

20 Box the corners of the bag. To do this, position the bag sideways so 1 side seam of the lining is centered at the bottom, forming a point.

21 Measure and mark a stitching line 2" (5 cm) from the point perpendicular to the seam. Sew on the marked line, and backstitch at each end to secure.

22 Leaving a ¼" (6 mm) seam, trim the point to get rid of excess bulk. Box all 4 corners.

23 Turn the bag right side out through the opening. Sew the opening shut.

24 Tuck the lining into the bag, and topstitch around the top edge of the bag.

FINISHED SIZE

24" × 68" (61 cm × 173 cm)

FINISHED BLOCK

6" × 9" (15 cm × 23 cm)

MATERIALS

Gray fabric, 1⅜ yard (1.3 m)
for top

Gray floral fabric, ¾ yard (0.7 m)
for top

Colorful prints, 5 fat quarters (each
18" × 21" [45.5 cm × 53.5 cm])
for top

Binding, ⅜ yard (0.3 m)

Batting, 28" × 72"
(71 cm × 183 cm)

Backing, 2 yards (1.8 m)

*All seams are ¼" (6 mm) unless
otherwise indicated.*

ON THE BEACH YOGA MAT

VIVIKA HANSEN DENEGRE

Simplicity and functionality make this yoga mat
a must-have for those who enjoy a sun salutation
at the beach or other outdoor venues. Fabric yoga
mats are soft on the feet, easy to carry, and can
be washed time and again.

CUTTING DIRECTIONS

To reduce the amount of stretch in the mat, cut the backing fabric so the long edge of the mat runs parallel to the selvedge. Label the pieces as you cut the fabric.

FROM THE GRAY FABRIC, CUT:

(7) 2½ (6.5 cm) × WOF (width-of-fabric) strips; subcut (28) 1½" × 2½" (3.8 cm × 6.5 cm) strips (label 1A)

(7) 2½ (6.5 cm) × WOF strips; subcut (28) 2½" (6.5 cm) squares (label 1C)

(7) 2½ (6.5 cm) × WOF strips; subcut (28) 2½" × 4¾" (6.5 cm × 12 cm) rectangles (label 1D)

(6) 3½" (9 cm) × WOF strips; subcut (56) 1½" × 3½" (3.8 cm × 9 cm) strips (label 2G)

(6) 3½" (9 cm) × WOF strips; subcut (28) 2¼" × 3½" (5.5 cm × 9 cm) rectangles (label 2H)

(6) 3½" (9 cm) × WOF strips; subcut (28) 1¼ × 3½" (3.2 cm × 9 cm) rectangles (label 2I)

(2) 3" (7.5 cm) × 24½" (62 cm) rectangles (top and bottom strips)

FROM THE GRAY FLORAL, CUT:

(2) 4½" (11.5 cm) × WOF strips; subcut (28) 2¼" × 4½" (5.5 cm × 11.5 cm) rectangles (label 1E)

(1) 3½" (9 cm) × WOF strips; subcut (28) 1½" × 3½" (3.8 cm × 9 cm) rectangles (label 2F)

(4) 2½" (6.5 cm) × WOF strips; subcut (28) 1½" × 2½" (3.8 cm × 6.5 cm) strips (label 3J)

(4) 2½" (6.5 cm) × WOF strips; subcut (28) 2½" × 4" (6.5 cm × 10 cm) strips (label 3L)

FROM THE COLORFUL PRINTS (MIX THE PRINTS), CUT:

(5) 2½" × 22" (6.5 cm × 56 cm) strips; subcut (28) 1¾" × 2½" (4.5 cm × 6.5 cm) rectangles (label 1B)

(5) 2½" × 22" (6.5 cm × 56 cm) strips; subcut (28) 2" × 2½" (5 cm × 6.5 cm) rectangles (label 3K)

FROM BACKING FABRIC, CUT:

(1) 28" × 72" (71 cm × 183 cm) rectangle

FROM BINDING, CUT:

(5) 2¼" (5.5 cm) × WOF strips

MAT CONSTRUCTION

Each block is made in 3 separate units that are joined to make the block. Finished blocks are sewn together in alternating positions (top up/top down) to give the illusion of a more complex design.

1 Unit 1: Starting with 1A and 1B, piece unit 1 in alphabetical order. Press the long seams toward pieces 1D and 1E (**Figure 1**). Make 28.

2 Unit 2: Starting with 2F and 2G, piece unit 2 in alphabetical order. Press the vertical seams toward pieces 2H and 2I (**Figure 2**). Make 28.

3 Unit 3: Piece together in alphabetical order. Press the seams toward 3K (**Figure 3**). Make 28.

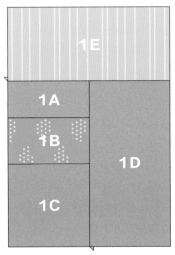

Fig. 1

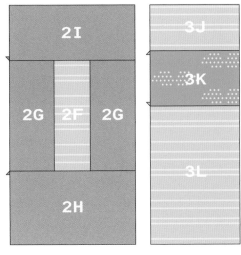

Fig. 2   Fig.3

4   Join 1 each of units 1–3 to make a block as shown (**Figure 4**). Make 28 blocks.

5   Arrange the blocks in 7 rows of 4 blocks each. Alternate the direction of the blocks top up/top down (**Figure 5**).

6   Sew the blocks into rows. Sew the rows together.

7   Add a 3" (7.5 cm) strip to both the top and the bottom to complete the yoga mat top. Press.

COMPLETE THE MAT

8   On a work surface, place the backing, wrong side up, then the batting, and then the quilt top, right side up. Baste.

9   Quilt as desired. I lengthened and widened a pre-programmed serpentine stitch on my home sewing machine and quilted the lines approximately ¼" (6 mm) apart.

10 Trim the edges.

11 Remove the selvedges from (5) 2¼" (5.5 cm) × WOF binding strips and sew them together with diagonal seams to create a straight-grain binding strip. Press the seams open. Fold the binding in half lengthwise, wrong sides together, and bind the mat (see French-Fold Binding in chapter 1 for directions).

TIP: *I like to use leftovers from the colorful fat quarters and gray floral fabrics to make the binding.*

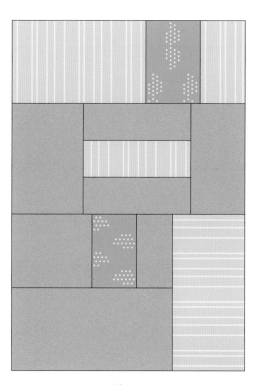

Fig. 4

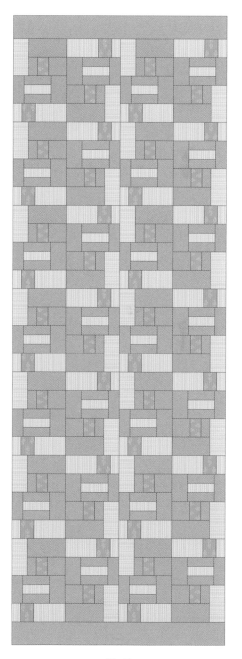

Fig. 5

15" × 17" (38 cm × 43 cm),
plus handles

MATERIALS

Canvas, ⅝ yard (0.6 m) for the
exterior

Quilting cotton, ⅝ yard (0.6 m) for
the lining

Batting, 7" (18 cm) square

Cotton strapping, 3 yards (2.7 m)
for the handles

*Use ½" (1.3 cm) seams unless
otherwise indicated.*

CANVAS TOTE

ROSEMARIE DEBOER

Too many tote bags? Never heard of such a thing.
Find some trendy fabric, and whip up a few for
yourself and your friends. A thoughtful design
feature encloses the side seams before the bag
is sewn together making the inside as beautiful
as the outside—with no extra steps!

CUTING DIRECTIONS

FROM THE CANVAS, CUT:

(2) 20" × 17" (51 cm × 43 cm) rectangles for the exterior

(1) 4½" × 7" (11.5 cm × 18 cm) rectangle for the pocket

FROM THE LINING FABRIC, CUT:

(1) 20" × 30" (51 cm × 76 cm) rectangle for the lining

(1) 7" × 10½" (18 cm × 26.5 cm) rectangle for the pocket

ASSEMBLE THE TOTE

1 Sew the short (20" [51 cm]) edges of the 2 exterior pieces with the right sides together. Press the seam open and lay flat, right side up.

2 With right sides together, place the lining piece on top of the exterior piece. Sew the 20" (51 cm) lining edges to the 20" (51 cm) exterior edges to create a tube. Press the seam toward the lining.

3 On a flat surface, smooth out the tube so that the bottom seam of the tote is centered. Pin.

NOTE: *Since the lining is cut shorter than the outer fabric, it will fold in to create the facing.*

4 Sew the sides of the lining and the canvas, leaving a 4" (10 cm) gap on 1 side for turning.

5 Turn the tote right side out through the opening.

TIP: *For crisp corners, do not clip them before turning the tote. Instead, fold 1 set of seams toward the lining. Holding them in place, fold the other set of seams over them. Keeping the seams firmly in place, turn the tote right side out, using your thumb to push the folded fabric into the corner. The fabric folds act like a stabilizer to keep the corners sharp.*

6 Edgestitch the opening to close it.

ADD POCKETS AND STRAPS

7 Sew the 7" (18 cm) edges of the pocket lining and the pocket exterior together with ¼" (6 mm) seams to create a tube. Turn right side out. Rotate the fabric so that 2½" (6.5 cm) of the exterior fabric is on the outside and the remainder forms an inside edge.

8 Slide the 7" (18 cm) square of batting into the tube. Trim the batting if necessary.

9 Center the top of the pocket 5½" (14 cm) down from the top edge of the tote. Pin it in place.

  NOTE: *The raw edges of the pocket will be covered by the strapping.*

10 Edgestitch the bottom of the pocket to the tote.

11 Measure 100" (254 cm) of strapping and join the ends with diagonal seams to create a large loop.

12 Spread the tote flat with the exterior right side up. With the diagonal join at 1 end, divide the strap in half and pin mark both points. Pin the marked straps to the bottom seam with a 7" (18 cm) gap between the centers of the straps (**Figure 1**).

  TIP: *To save yourself grief, make sure that when you fold the tote in half, the handle portions are exactly the same length. This is important so you don't end up with uneven straps. Make adjustments now.*

13 Pin the strap in place, covering the raw edges of the pocket with the edges of the strap. Sew the strap to the tote along both sides.

14 Reinforce the strap by making a boxstitch at the top edge of the tote (**Figure 2**).

FINISH THE TOTE

15 With right sides together, sew the sides of the tote together.

16 To box the corners and give the tote some depth, align the side seam with the bottom seam. Measure in 2" (5 cm) from the tip and stitch perpendicular to the seam. Repeat on the other corner (**Figure 3**). Turn the tote right side out.

  TIP: *Do not trim off the point. Push it toward the base for extra stability.*

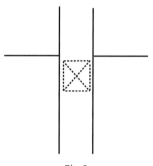

Fig. 2

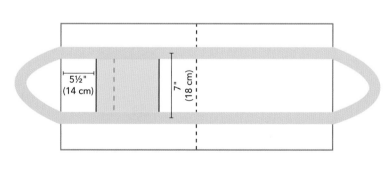

Fig. 1

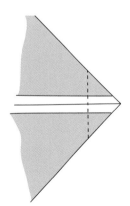

Fig. 3

FINISHED SIZE

Fits a 5½" × 8" (14 cm × 20.5 cm) softcover sketchbook

MATERIALS

Neutrals prints, 15 charm squares (5" [12.5 cm] each) or scraps for cover

Orange, 1 charm square (5" [12.5 cm]) for cover

Lime, 1 charm square (5" [12.5 cm]) for cover

Soft blue prints, 4 fat eighths (11" × 18" [28 cm × 45.5 cm] each) or scraps for cover

Navy, fat eighth (11" × 18" [28 cm × 45.5 cm]) for binding

Lightweight, woven fusible interfacing, 15" × 21" (38 cm × 53.5 cm)

Embroidery floss, blue and yellow, 1 yard (0.9 cm) each

Softcover sketchbook, 5½" × 8" (14 cm × 20.5 cm)

All seams are ¼" (6 mm) unless otherwise indicated.

SKETCHBOOK COVER

LEE CHAPPELL MONROE

This journal's miniature patchwork is a great use for your favorite scraps, as well as a way to start dabbling with trendy big-stitch quilting.

CUTTING DIRECTIONS

NOTE: *Trim the fusible interfacing to 12½" × 20¾" (31.5 cm × 52.5 cm)*

FROM NEUTRAL FABRICS, CUT:

(56) 1¼" × 2¾" (3.2 cm × 7 cm) rectangles

(56) 1¼" (3.2 cm) squares

FROM LIME CHARM SQUARES, CUT:

(4) 1¼" (3.2 cm) squares

FROM ORANGE CHARM SQUARES, CUT:

(4) 1¼" × 2¾" (3.2 cm) rectangles

FROM SOFT BLUE PRINTS, CUT:

(64) 1¼" × 2¾" (3.2 cm × 7 cm) rectangles

FROM NAVY FABRIC, CUT:

(2) 2" × 13" (5 cm × 33 cm) strips

CREATE THE COVER

1 Sew a neutral square to a neutral rectangle. Make 56 units.

2 Sew 4 units together to make a column (**Figure 1**). Make 14 columns. Press the seams toward the end of the column with the square.

3 Alternating the rectangles and squares as the starting point, sew the columns together. Make 1 section with 11 columns and a second section with 3 columns.

4 Sew the narrow ends of 4 blue rectangles together. Press the seams in 1 direction. Make 16 rows.

5 Sew the rows together, nesting the seams.

6 Make 1 row alternating the orange rectangles with the lime squares. Press the seams toward the end of the block with the lime square.

7 Follow **Figure 2** to sew the units together.

8 With 6 strands of embroidery floss, make cross stitches in the squares and colors as shown.

9 Press the fusible interfacing to the back of the pieced cover.

FINISH THE COVER

10 Press the navy strips in half lengthwise to create binding. Fold the raw edges toward the pressed center crease and press again.

11 Bind each of the narrow raw edges of the pieced cover (see French-Fold Binding in chapter 1 for tips). Trim the ends of the binding.

12 With the right side of the piece facing up, fold in 3" (7.5 cm) from each edge with right sides together.

13 On both sides of the book flap, stitch 1⅝" (4 cm) from the top and bottom edges through the folded layers. Backstitch at the binding and the folded edge.

14 Turn the cover right side out. Slide the sketchbook into the pockets.

Fig. 1

Fig. 2

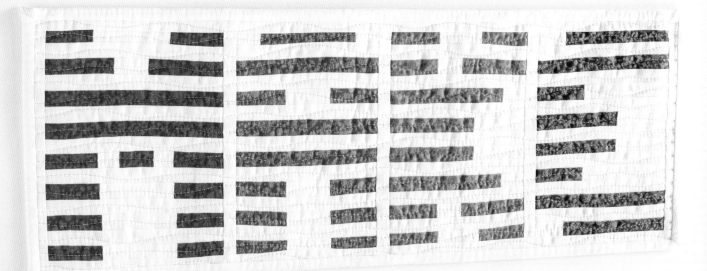

FINISHED SIZE

8½" × 26½"
(21.5 cm × 67.5 cm)

MATERIALS

Pink fabric, 10" (25.5 cm) square

Orange fabric, 10" (25.5 cm) square

Green fabric, 10" (25.5 cm) square

Blue fabric, 10" (25.5 cm) square

White fabric, ½ yard (0.5 m)

Backing, ½ yard (0.5 m)

Binding, ¼ yard (0.2 m)

Batting, 12" × 32"
(30.5 cm × 81.5 cm)

All seams are ¼" (6 mm) unless otherwise indicated.

MAKE MINI QUILT

ANGELA BOWMAN

This mini quilt is a fantastic scrap-buster. Four blocks spelling "MAKE" are created with 1" (2.5 cm) strips in place. The quilt is inspired by the wonderfully geeky and 80's-inspired font, "Edit Undo," by Brian Kent.

CUTTING DIRECTIONS

Label each piece as you cut with the noted letter.

TIP: *Cutting WOF strips and then subcutting the smaller pieces will save time.*

FROM PINK FABRIC, CUT:

(2) 2½" × 4" (6.5 cm × 10 cm) rectangles (M1)

(2) 1" × 7" (2.5 cm × 18 cm) strips (M2)

(2) 1" × 3¼" (2.5 cm × 8.5 cm) strips (M3)

(2) 1" × 2½" (2.5 cm × 6.5 cm) strips (M4)

(1) 1" × 1¾" (2.5 cm × 4.5 cm) rectangles (M5)

FROM ORANGE FABRIC, CUT:

(2) 2½ × 4" (6.5 cm × 10 cm) rectangles (A1)

(3) 1" × 6¼" (2.5 cm × 16 cm) strips (A2)

(1) 1" × 4¼" (2.5 cm × 11 cm) strips (A3)

FROM GREEN FABRIC, CUT:

(1) 2" × 5¼" (5 cm × 13.5 cm) strips (K1)

(1) 2" × 4" (5 cm × 10 cm) strips (K2)

(1) 2" × 3¼" (5 cm × 8.5 cm) strips (K3)

(3) 2" × 2½" (5 cm × 6.5 cm) rectangles (K4)

FROM BLUE FABRIC, CUT:

(1) 2" × 5" (5 cm × 12.5 cm) strips (E1)

(1) 2" × 4" (5 cm × 10 cm) strips (E2)

(1) 2" × 2½" (5 cm × 6.5 cm) rectangles (E3)

(2) 1" × 6¼" (2.5 cm × 16 cm) strips (E4)

FROM THE WHITE FABRIC STRIP, CUT:

(1) 3¼" × 4" (8.5 cm × 10 cm) rectangles (M6)

(1) 1" × 1¾" (2.5 cm × 4.5 cm) rectangles (M7)

(2) 1" × 1¼" (2.5 cm × 3.2 cm) rectangles (M8)

(7) 1" × 7¼" (2.5 cm × 18.5 cm) rectangles (M)

(1) 2¼" × 4" (5.5 cm × 10 cm) rectangle (A4)

(2) 1" × 1½" (2.5 cm × 3.8 cm) rectangles (A5)

(2) 1½" × 2" (3.8 cm × 5 cm) rectangles (K5)

(1) 1¾" × 2" (4.5 cm × 5 cm) rectangle (E7)

(1) 2" × 2¼" (5 cm × 5.5 cm) rectangle (K6)

(2) 2" × 2¾" (5 cm × 7 cm) rectangles (K7, E5)

(1) 2" × 4¼" (5 cm × 11 cm) rectangle (E6)

(21) 1" × 6¼" (2.5 cm × 16 cm) strips (7 each of A, K, E)

(5) 1" × 9" (2.5 cm × 23 cm) strips for sashing/side borders

(2) 1" × 29" (2.5 cm × 73.5 cm) strips for top/bottom borders

(2) 2½" (6.5 cm) × WOF (width-of-fabric) strips for binding

PREPARE THE BLOCKS

Refer to Figure 1 throughout block assembly.

1   Following the diagram for each letter, create the
    strip sets for each block. Arrange the pieced strips
    and 7½" (19 cm) strips for each letter on a design
    wall.

    TIP: *Each letter is made from 15 strips.*

2   Sew the rows together in pairs: Row 1 to row 2,
    row 3 to row 4, etc. Sew the paired rows together.
    Press the seams open.

    TIP: *Pin every 1–2" (2.5–5 cm) to keep these thin
    strips straight while sewing. Take care not to pull on
    the fabric, but let the feed dogs to their job.*

Fig. 1

Arrange the pieces | Make the strip sets | Subcut the 1" (2.5 cm) strips | Assemble the letter block — K

Arrange the pieces | Make the strip sets | Subcut the 1" (2.5 cm) strips | Assemble the letter block — E

Fig. 1 (continued)

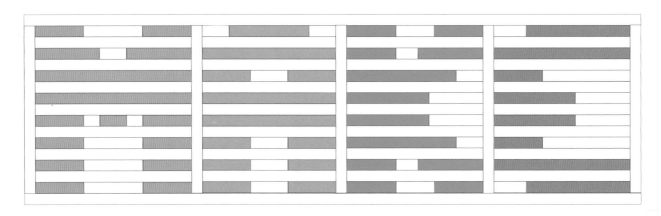

Fig. 2

QUILT CONSTRUCTION

3 Following **Figure 2**, arrange the letter blocks with the 1" × 9" (2.5 cm × 23 cm) sashing strips and 1" × 29" (2.5 cm × 73.5 cm) top and bottom border strips as shown. Working from one side to the other, sew the sashing strips to the letters connecting the blocks. Sew the top and bottom borders to the mini quilt top.

FINISH THE QUILT

4 Layer the backing wrong side up, followed by the batting, and then the quilt top right side up. Baste.

5 Quilt as desired. The quilt shown here was quilted with horizontal wavy lines.

6 Join the 2½" (6.5 cm) binding strips with diagonal seams to make one long binding strip. Fold in half lengthwise and bind the quilt (see French-Fold Binding in chapter 1 for directions).

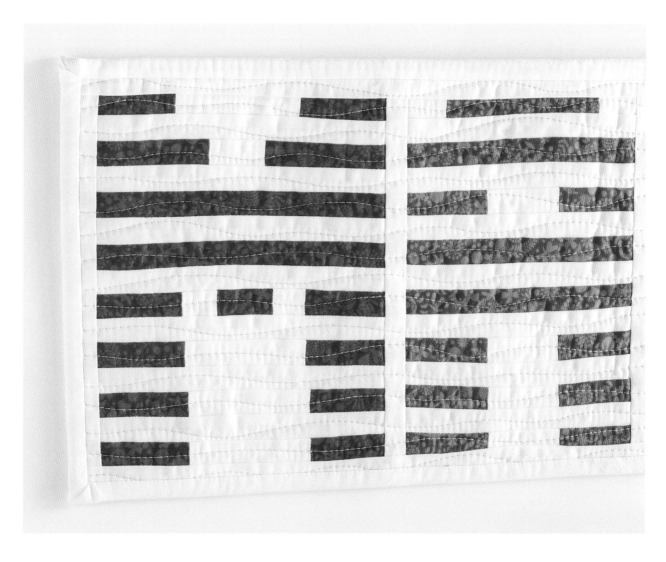

3

QUILTS

FRESH DESIGNS AND CONTEMPORARY FABRIC FOR A MODERN TAKE ON THE BELOVED QUILT FORM

Refer to chapter 1: Quilting Basics for instructions on a variety of the quilting techniques found in this book.

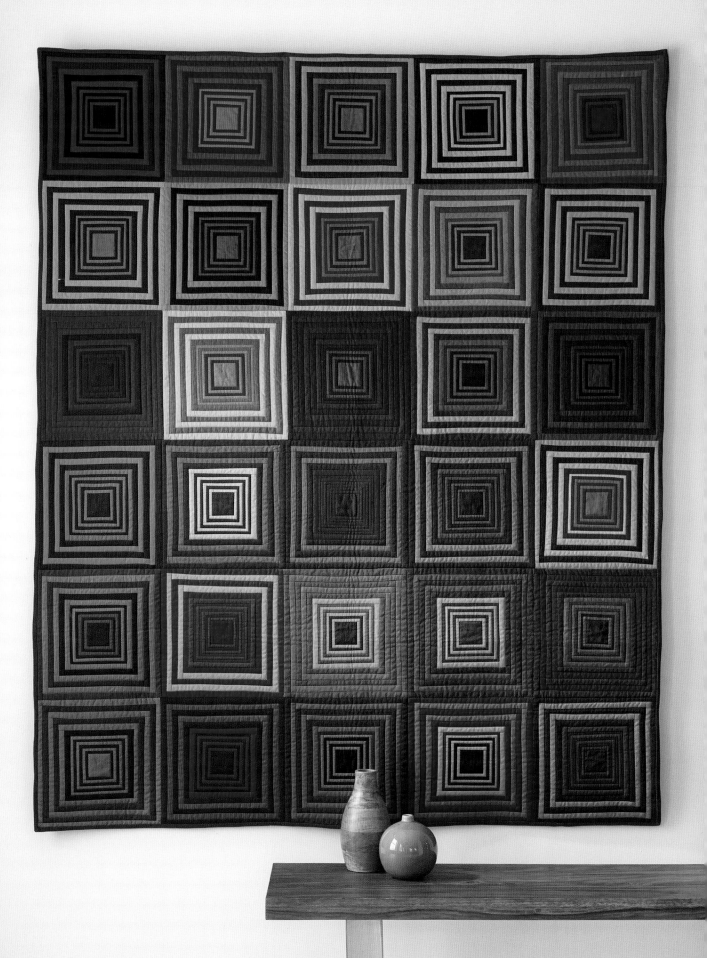

FINISHED QUILT SIZE

55½" × 66½" (141 cm × 169 cm)

FINISHED BLOCK SIZE

11" (28 cm) square

MATERIALS

Assorted light and dark solid fabrics, approximately 3 yards (2.7 m) light and 3 yards (2.7 m) dark

Backing, 3½ yards (3.2 m)

Low-loft batting, 63" × 72" (160 cm × 183 cm) or twin size

Binding, ½ yard (0.5 m)

OPTIONAL

12½" (31.5 cm) square acrylic ruler

All seams are ¼" (6 mm) unless otherwise indicated.

MODERN LOG CABIN QUILT

TARA FAUGHNAN

Illustrations by Tara Faughnan

This is a great quilt for beginners and more experienced quilters alike. It is simple to piece yet leaves a lot of room for playing with color. The instructions are given using four different colors. Once you are comfortable with the basic piecing for this block, feel free to experiment with your own color combinations.

CUTTING DIRECTIONS

Cutting instructions are for 1 block measuring 11½" (29 cm) square (11" [28 cm] square finished size).

For each block choose 4 different solid fabrics. Label them A, B, C, and D (**Figure 1**). Cut the strips the width-of-fabric (WOF) so you have a long piece of fabric to work with. Do not piece the strips. Set aside the leftover parts of the strips to use in another block.

FROM FABRIC A, CUT:

(1) 2½" (6.5 cm) square

(2) ¾" (2 cm) × WOF strips (total length needed 51" [129.5 cm])

FROM FABRIC B, CUT:

(2) ¾" (2 cm) × WOF strips (total length needed 45" [114.5 cm])

FROM FABRIC C, CUT:

(3) 1" (2.5 cm) × WOF strips (total length needed 96" [244 cm])

FROM FABRIC D, CUT:

(3) 1" (2.5 cm) × WOF strips (total length needed 108" [274 cm])

Save Time

Instead of cutting the strips to size for each round, you can work with one long strip of fabric. Align the strip to the block, sew, and then trim off the excess.

ASSEMBLE THE BLOCKS

Accuracy is critical when sewing this block so it is highly recommended to make a test block to check your piecing and seam allowances. If your block is too small, make your seam allowance slightly less than ¼" (6 mm). Conversely, if your block is too large, make the seam allowance slightly wider than ¼" (6 mm). You can use a 12½" (31.5 cm) square ruler to check the size of the block as you go, and adjust seam allowances accordingly.

NOTE: *After sewing each pair of strips, press seams away from the center.*

1   Referring to **Figure 2**, sew a 2½" (6.5 cm) strip of fabric B to the top and bottom of the 2½" (6.5 cm) fabric A square. Sew a 3" (7.5 cm) strip of fabric B to each side.

2   Sew a 3" (7.5 cm) strip of fabric A to the top and bottom of the block. Sew a 3½" (9 cm) strip of fabric A to each side.

3   Sew a 3½" (9 cm) strip of fabric B to the top and bottom. Sew a 4" (10 cm) strip of fabric B to each side.

4   Sew a 4" (10 cm) strip of fabric A to the top and bottom. Sew a 4½" (11.5 cm) strip of fabric A to each side.

5   Sew a 4½" (11 cm) strip of fabric B to the top and bottom. Sew a 5" (12.5 cm) strip of fabric B to each side.

6   Sew a 5" (12.5 cm) strip of fabric A to the top and bottom. Sew a 5½" (14 cm) strip of fabric A to each side.

NOTE: *At this point your block should measure 5½" (14 cm) square. Measure and adjust seam allowances as necessary.*

7   Sew a 5½" (14 cm) strip of fabric C to the top and bottom. Sew a 6½" (16.5 cm) strip of fabric C to each side.

8   Sew a 6½" (16.5 cm) strip of fabric D to the top and bottom. Sew a 7½" (19 cm) strip of fabric D to each side.

9   Sew a 7½" (19 cm) strip of fabric C to the top and bottom. Sew an 8½" (21.5 cm) strip of fabric C to each side.

10 Sew an 8½" (21.5 cm) strip of fabric D to the top and bottom. Sew a 9½" (24 cm) strip of fabric D to each side.

11 Sew a 9½" (24 cm) strip of fabric C to the top and bottom. Sew a 10½" (26.5 cm) strip of fabric C to each side.

12 Sew a 10½" (26.5 cm) strip of fabric D to the top and bottom. Sew an 11½" (29 cm) strip of fabric D to each side.

13 Square your block up to measure 11½" (29 cm) square.

14 Make 30 blocks.

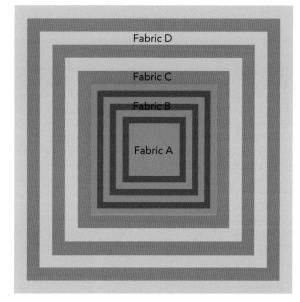

Fig. 1

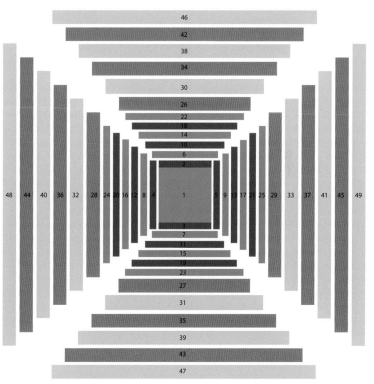

Add strips in number order as shown here.

Fig. 2

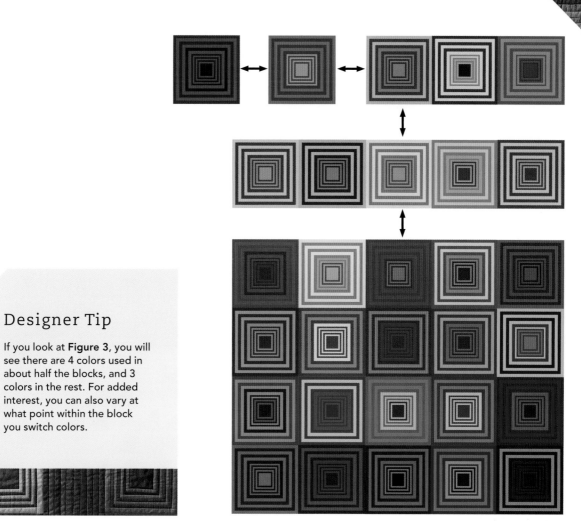

Fig. 3

Designer Tip

If you look at **Figure 3**, you will see there are 4 colors used in about half the blocks, and 3 colors in the rest. For added interest, you can also vary at what point within the block you switch colors.

ASSEMBLE THE QUILT

15 Referring to **Figure 3**, sew 5 blocks together to make a row. Make 6 rows and sew them together.

16 Trim the batting to 60" × 70" (152 cm × 178 cm).

17 Cut the backing fabric in half. Trim off the selvedges and sew the halves together along the trimmed edge. Press the seam open.

18 Layer the backing wrong side up, followed by the batting, and then the quilt top, right side up. Baste the layers together using the method of your choice.

19 Quilt in the ditch or as desired. Bind the quilt using your preferred method. (See French-Fold Binding in chapter 1 for directions.)

FINISHED SIZE

54" × 60" (137 cm × 152.5 cm)

FINISHED BLOCK SIZE

8" (20.5 cm) square

MATERIALS

Assorted solids and prints in
blacks and dark grays, 1¼ yards
(1.1 m) total

Gold fabric, fat eighth (11" × 18"
[28 cm × 45.5 cm])

Light gray fabric, fat eighth
(11" × 18" [28 cm × 45.5 cm])

White fabric, 3¼ yards (3 m)

Backing fabric, 3½ yards (3.2 m)

Binding fabric, ½ yard (0.5 m)

Batting, twin-size

*All seams are ¼" (6 mm) unless
otherwise indicated.*

FLY
AWAY
QUILT

SUZY WILLIAMS

Illustrations by Suzy Williams

Inspired by a Gee's Bend quilt called "Birds
In Flight" by Mertlene Perkins, this quilt uses
negative space and subtle changes in color to
create a delicate composition. By scattering some
triangles, the "birds" appear to be flying away
from the flock.

CUTTING DIRECTIONS

FROM BLACK AND DARK GRAY FABRIC, CUT:

(20) 5¾" (14.5 cm) squares

(47) 2⅞" (7.5 cm) squares; subcut on the diagonal (94 triangles total)

FROM GOLD FABRIC, CUT:

(1) 5¾" (14.5 cm) square

(2) 2⅞" (7.5 cm) squares; subcut on the diagonal (4 triangles total)

FROM LIGHT GRAY FABRIC, CUT:

(1) 5¾" (14.5 cm) square

(2) 2⅞" (7.5 cm) squares; subcut on the diagonal (4 triangles total)

FROM WHITE FABRIC, CUT:

(23) 5¾" (14.5 cm) squares

(13) 8⅞" (23 cm) squares; subcut on the diagonal (26 squares total)

(6) 2½" (6.5 cm) squares

(3) 2½" × 4½" (6.5 cm × 11.5 cm) rectangles

(1) 2½" × 5½" (6.5 cm × 14 cm) rectangle

(2) 2½" × 6½" (6.5 cm × 16.5 cm) rectangles

(2) 2½" × 8½" (6.5 cm × 21.5 cm) rectangles

(1) 8½" × 16½" (21.5 cm × 42 cm) rectangle

(1) 7½" × 19½" (19 cm × 49.5 cm) rectangle

(1) 7½" × 39½" (19 cm × 100.5 cm) rectangle

(1) 7½" × 40½" (19 cm × 103 cm) rectangle

(3) 7½" (19 cm) × WOF (width-of-fabric) strips

FROM BINDING, CUT:

(7) 2¼" (5.5 cm) × WOF strips

MAKE THE HALF-SQUARE TRIANGLES (HSTS)

1   On the wrong side of the 5¾" (14.5 cm) white squares, draw diagonal lines (**Figure 1**).

2   With right sides together, pair a black/dark gray square with a marked white square.

3   Sew ¼" (6 mm) on both sides of each of the diagonal lines (**Figure 2**).

4   Cut along the marked lines, and again at the center vertical and horizontal lines, creating 8 HSTs (**Figure 3**).

5   Press seams to the darker fabric. Trim the dog ears (**Figure 4**).

6   Make the following HSTs: 155 black/dark gray, 10 gold, and 8 light gray.

ASSEMBLE THE BLOCK

7   For each block, assemble 6 HSTs and 4 black triangles as shown. Sew the units into columns, and then sew the columns together (**Figure 5**).

TIP: Press the seams in each column in the opposite direction as the adjacent row, allowing the seams to nest.

8   Place 1 white triangle, right sides together, on top of an HST unit. Line up the diagonal, pin, and sew. Press the seam open.

NOTE: *The diagonal seam is on the bias. Take care not to stretch it as you work.*

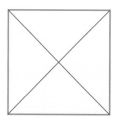

Fig. 1

Fig. 2

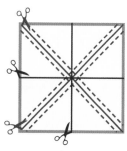

Fig. 3

Fig. 4

Fig. 5

9   Make 25 blocks. (Refer to **Figure 7** as a color guide, if desired.)

10 Arrange the 3 remaining "flight" blocks on a design wall. Sew the units into rows. Sew the rows together (**Figure 6**).

    NOTE: *One gold HST will be left over for the border.*

ASSEMBLE THE QUILT TOP

11 Assemble the blocks into rows. Sew the rows together.

12 Sew the remaining gold HST to the 2½" × 5½" (6.5 cm × 14 cm) strip.

13 Sew the 7½" (19 cm) × WOF strips together. Cut into 2 smaller border strips: 7½" × 47½" (19 cm × 120.5 cm) and 7½" × 53½" (19 cm × 136 cm).

14 Follow **Figure 7** to add the white borders.

COMPLETE THE QUILT

15 Divide the backing into (2) 1¾ yards (1.6 m) lengths. Sew panels together lengthwise.

16 Layer the backing wrong side up, followed by the batting, and then the quilt top, right side up. Baste.

16 Quilt as desired. The featured design has straight-line quilting.

17 Join the binding strips with diagonal seams to create a straight grain binding strip. Fold the strip in half lengthwise and bind the quilt (see French-Fold Binding chapter 1 for directions).

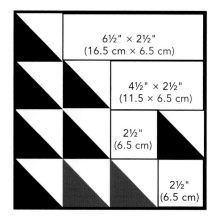
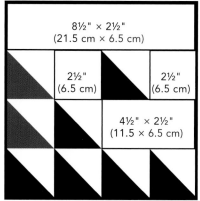
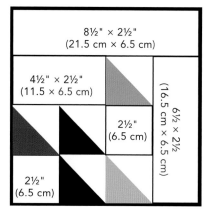

Fig. 6

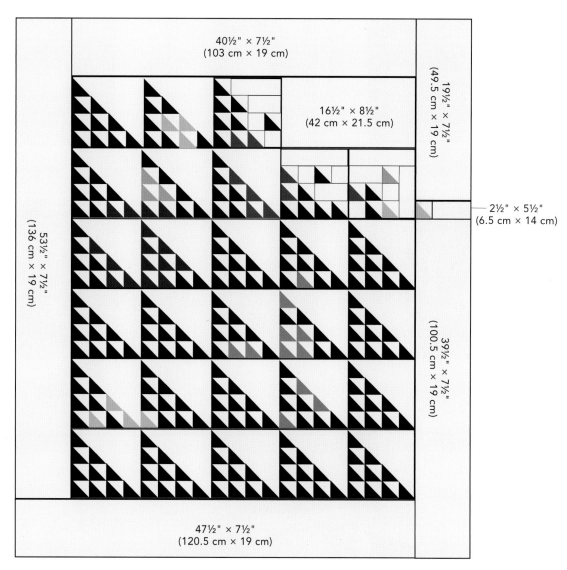

Fig. 7

FINISHED SIZE

52" (132 cm) square

FINISHED BLOCK SIZE

12" (30.5 cm) square

MATERIALS

Assorted plaids, (9) 5" (12.5 cm) squares

Assorted solids, 9 sets of (8) coordinating 5" (12.5 cm) squares (72 squares total)

Assorted gray/white prints, 8 fat quarters (18" × 21" [45.5 cm × 53.5 cm])

Backing fabric, 3½ (3.2 m) yards

Facing or binding fabric, ½ yard (0.5 m)

Batting, twin-size

All seams are ¼" (6 mm) unless otherwise indicated.

MODULE QUILT

CHRISTINE BARNES

Despite its ultra simplicity, Christine Barnes' quilt packs a punch. For maximum color impact she advises, "Don't be afraid to include colors that aren't in the center plaid square—they add a surprise element and make your design more original. Also, place solid squares of similar value and color side by side in the blocks. These create new shapes and modernize the classic Nine Patch."

CUTTING DIRECTIONS

Measurements include ¼" (6 mm) seam allowances. Border and sashing strips are the exact length needed. You may want to make them longer to allow for piecing variations.

FROM EACH ASSORTED PLAID 5" (12.5 CM) SQUARE, CUT:

(1) 4½" (11.5 cm) square

FROM EACH ASSORTED SOLID 5" (12.5 CM) SQUARE, CUT:

(1) 4½" (11.5 cm) square

FROM ASSORTED LIGHT GRAY/WHITE PRINT FAT QUARTERS, CUT:

4½"-wide (11.5 cm) strips ranging in length from 4½–18½" (11.5–47 cm) long for sashing and borders

FROM BINDING FABRIC, CUT:

(5) 2¼"-wide (5.5 cm) strips for facing (or binding)

BLOCK ASSEMBLY

1   Referring to **Figure 1**, arrange 1 plaid square and 8 coordinating solid squares. Sew the blocks into rows; sew the rows together to complete 1 block.

2   Make 9 blocks.

PIECED SASHING AND BORDER STRIPS ASSEMBLY

Refer to **Figure 2** throughout quilt top assembly.

3   Sew the assorted gray/white sashing strips to make (1) 4½" × 12½" (11.5 cm × 31.5 cm) pieced vertical sashing strip. Make 6 sashing strips.

4   In a similar manner, make (2) 4½" × 44½" (11.5 cm × 113 cm) pieced horizontal sashing strips, (2) 4½" × 44½" (11.5 cm × 113 cm) pieced side borders, and (2) 4½" × 52½" (11.5 cm × 133.5 cm) pieced top and bottom borders.

QUILT ASSEMBLY

5   Arrange the blocks and the vertical and horizontal sashing strips, as shown.

6   Sew the blocks and sashing strips into rows; sew the rows with the horizontal sashing strips to complete the quilt center.

7   Sew the pieced side borders to the quilt center. Sew the pieced top and bottom borders to the quilt.

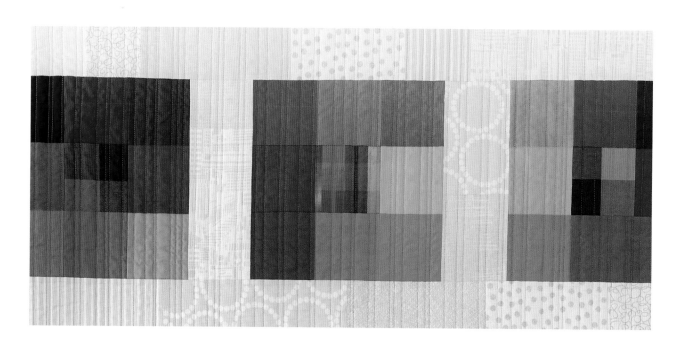

FINISHING

8 Divide backing into (2) 60" (152.5 cm) pieces. Cut 1 piece in half to make 2 narrow panels. Sew 1 narrow panel to each side of the wider panel; press seam allowances open. Trim the backing to 60" (152.5 cm) square.

9 Layer the backing, batting, and the quilt top; baste. Quilt as desired. The quilt shown here was quilted with randomly spaced vertical lines.

10 Sew 2¼"-wide (5.5 cm) binding strips into 1 continuous piece and finish the quilt using a facing or by binding (see French-Fold binding chapter 1 for directions).

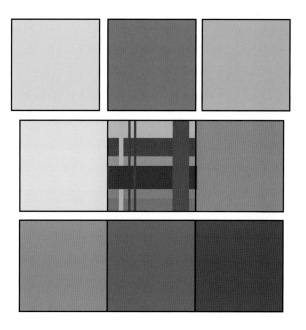

Fig. 1

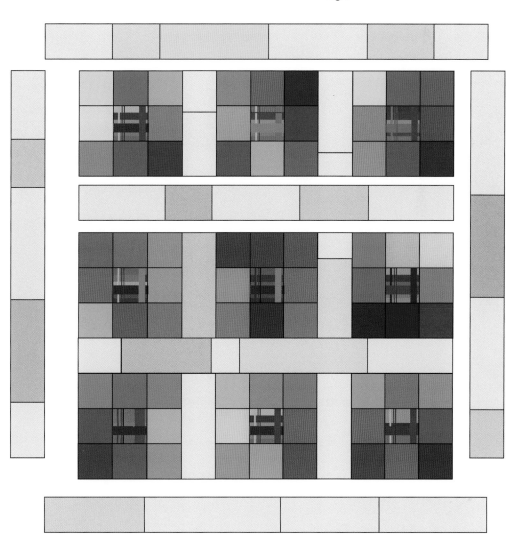

Fig. 2

FINISHED SIZE

63" (160 cm) square

FINISHED BLOCK SIZE

7" (18 cm) square

MATERIALS

Solid in mustard, ⅜ yard (0.3 m)

Chocolate brown, raspberry, coral pink, grass green, chartreuse, and indigo blue solids, ⅝ yard (0.6 m) each

Orange, red, pale blue, and turquoise solids, ⅞ yard (0.8 m) each

Backing, 4¾ yards (4.3 m) for backing and facing strips

Batting, twin-size

NOTE: *The fabrics used in this quilt were all hand dyed by the artist.*

All seams are ¼" (6 mm) unless otherwise indicated.

THROUGH THE BLINDS QUILT

MALKA DUBRAWSKY

It's a cliché—though essentially true—that simple things are often the best. This adage definitely applies to this quilt design. Crafted from the most basic of building blocks—half-square triangles—this quilt has a graphic, intense impact, intermixing strong colors and a purposeful use of value. These elements combine to create a quilt that is bold and beautiful, yet quick to sew.

CUTTING DIRECTIONS

FROM MUSTARD FABRIC, CUT:

(4) 8½" (21.5 cm) squares

FROM INDIGO BLUE FABRIC, CUT:

(5) 8½" (21.5 cm) squares

FROM CHOCOLATE BROWN, RASPBERRY, CORAL PINK, AND CHARTREUSE FABRIC, CUT FROM EACH:

(6) 8½" (21.5 cm) squares

FROM GRASS GREEN FABRIC, CUT:

(8) 8½" (21.5 cm) squares

FROM RED FABRIC, CUT:

(9) 8½" (21.5 cm) squares

FROM ORANGE AND PALE BLUE FABRIC, CUT FROM EACH:

(10) 8½" (21.5 cm) squares

FROM TURQUOISE FABRIC, CUT:

(11) 8½" (21.5 cm) squares

FROM BACKING FABRIC, CUT:

(7) 3" (7.5 cm) × WOF (width-of-fabric) strips for facing

Divide remaining backing in half for quilt backing.

HST ASSEMBLY

1 Referring to the Half-Squares Triangle blocks two-at-a-time directions in chapter 1, make 81 total half-square triangles (HSTs) from the following combination of squares:

NOTE: *There will be extra HSTs.*

4 red/orange pairs

5 pale blue/raspberry pairs

4 pale blue/turquoise pairs

5 coral pink/red pairs

5 chartreuse/grass green pairs

3 mustard/grass green pairs

6 orange/chocolate brown pairs

6 turquoise/indigo blue pairs

1 chartreuse/pale blue pair

1 mustard/turquoise pair

1 coral pink/raspberry pair

2 Trim each HST block to 7½" (19 cm) square.

QUILT ASSEMBLY

3 Referring to **Figure 1**, arrange the HSTs as shown.

4 For ease of construction, sew HSTs into Nine-Patch blocks.

5 Sew the Nine-Patch blocks into rows. Sew the rows together to complete the quilt top.

FINISHING

6 Divide backing into (2) 2-yard (1.8 m) lengths. Sew panels lengthwise.

7 Layer backing, batting, and quilt top; baste. Quilt as desired. Quilt shown was quilted with horizontal matchstick quilting approximately ¼" (6 mm) apart.

8 Finish the quilt using 3" (7.5 cm) facing strips to give the edge an ultra-modern look.

Fig. 1

FINISHED SIZE

60" × 72" (152.5 cm × 183 cm)

MATERIALS

Gray fabric for blocks, 2¼ (2.1 m) yards

Orange fabric for blocks, 1⅜ yards (1.3 m)

Aqua fabric for blocks, 1¼ yard (1.1 m)

Lavender fabric for blocks, 1 yard (0.9 m)

Burgundy fabric for blocks, ¾ yard (0.7 m)

Backing, 3¾ yards (3.4 m)

Binding fabric, ⅝ yard (0.6 m)

Batting, 68" × 80" (173 cm × 203 cm)

Template plastic or cardboard

Urban Trek templates (see Templates section)

All seams are ¼ " (6 mm) unless otherwise indicated.

URBAN TREK QUILT

HEATHER BLACK

This quilt was inspired by the designer's love of bold color combinations and geometric design. The quilt draws on the shapes and textures encountered on a walk in the city—crosswalks, manhole covers, traffic signs, and construction sites. The pattern is based on an oversized Drunkard's Path template—another unexpected element.

CUTTING DIRECTIONS

Measurements include ¼" (6 mm) seam allowances. Make templates from the patterns in the Templates section. Label the templates and pieces as you cut.

FROM GRAY FABRIC, CUT:

(2) 6½" × 40" (16.5 cm × 101.5 cm) strips; subcut (1) 6½" × 22½" (16.5 cm × 57 cm) H rectangle, (2) 6½" × 12½" (16.5 cm × 31.5 cm) G rectangles, and (12) 1½" × 6½" (3.8 cm × 16.5 cm) A rectangles

(2) 12½" × 40" (31.5 cm × 101.5 cm) strips; subcut (1) 12½" (31.5 cm) M square, (1) 12½" × 22½" (31.5 cm × 57 cm) K rectangle, and (17) 1½" x 12½" (3.8 cm × 31.5 cm) C rectangles

(12) 2½" × 40" (6.5 cm × 101.5 cm) strips; subcut (12) 2½" × 30½" (6.5 cm × 77.5 cm) D strips

FROM ORANGE FABRIC, CUT:

(2) 12½" × 40" (31.5 cm × 101.5 cm) strips; subcut (19) 1½" × 12½" (3.8 cm × 31.5 cm) C rectangles, and 5 using template B

NOTE: *Nest the B templates for the most efficient use of fabric.*

(2) 6½" × 40" (16.5 cm × 101.5 cm) strips; subcut (1) 6½" × 24½" (16.5 cm × 62 cm) I rectangle, and (24) 1½" × 6½" (3.8 cm × 16.5 cm) A rectangles.

(2) 1½" × 40" (3.8 cm × 101.5 cm) strips. From strips, cut (5) 1½" × 10½" (3.8 cm × 26.5 cm) B rectangles.

FROM AQUA FABRIC, CUT:

(12) 2½" × 40" (6.5 cm × 101.5 cm) strips. Trim strips to 2½" × 30½" (6.5 cm × 77.5 cm) for D.

(1) using template A

FROM LAVENDER FABRIC, CUT:

(1) 12½" × 40" (31.5 cm × 101.5 cm) strip; subcut 1 using template A, 1 using template B, (1) 6½" × 12½" (16.5 cm × 31.5 cm) G rectangle, (1) 3½" × 12½" (9 cm × 31.5 cm) F rectangle, (1)1½" × 12½" (3.8 cm × 31.5 cm) C rectangle.

(1) 11½" × 40" (29 cm × 101.5 cm) strip. Trim strip to 11½" × 30½" (29 cm × 77.5 cm) for J.

(1) 6½" × 40" (16.5 cm × 101.5 cm) strip; subcut (12) 1½" × 6½" (3.8 cm × 16.5 cm) A rectangles, and (1) 3½" × 6½" (9 cm × 16.5 cm) E rectangle.

(2) 1½" × 40" (3.8 cm × 101.5 cm) strips; subcut (5) 1½" × 10½" (3.8 cm × 26.5 cm) B rectangles.

FROM BURGUNDY FABRIC, CUT:

(2) 12" × 40" (30.5 cm × 101.5 cm) strips. From strips, cut 5 using template A.

FROM THE BINDING FABRIC, CUT:

(7) 2¼" (5.5 cm) × WOF (width-of-fabric) strips.

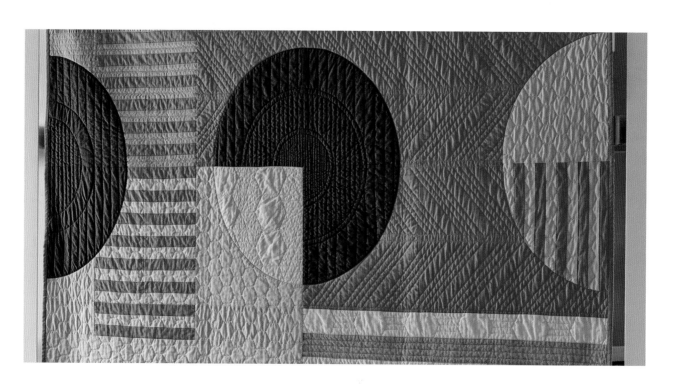

ASSEMBLE SECTION A

1 Sew 6 orange C strips to 6 gray C strips, alternating colors (**Figure 1**). The finished block will measure 12½" (31.5 cm) square.

   TIP: *Reverse the direction of sewing with each strip to prevent bowing. After sewing and pressing the first 2 strips, test the ¼" (6 mm) seam allowance. The strip should measure 2½" (6.5 cm) wide. Adjust your seam allowance if necessary.*

2 Sew 3 aqua D strips to 3 gray D strips, alternating colors (**Figure 2**).

3 Sew the gray G rectangle to the left side of the gray/orange strip unit. Sew the gray M square to the left of the aqua/gray strip unit. Sew the sections together to complete section A (**Figure 3**).

ASSEMBLE SECTION B

4 Sew 6 lavender A strips to 6 orange A strips, alternating colors. Make 2 units (**Figure 4**).

5 Sew 6 orange A strips to 6 gray A strips, alternating colors. Make 2 units (**Figure 5**).

6 Sew 1 of the lavender/orange units to a lavender G rectangle (**Figure 6**). The finished unit will measure 12½" (31.5 cm) square.

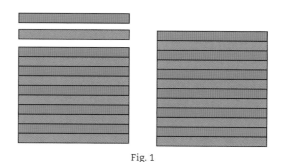

Fig. 1

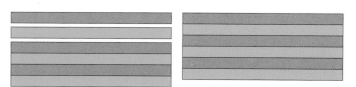

Fig. 2

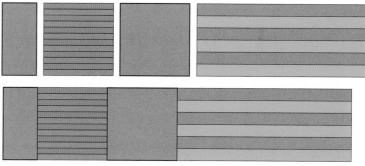

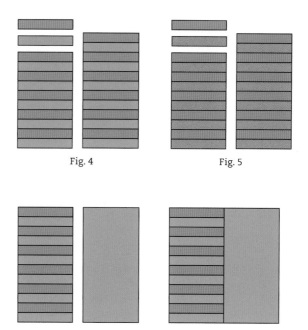

Fig. 3

Fig. 4　　　　Fig. 5

Fig. 6

7 Sew 1 of the orange/gray units to a gray G rectangle. The finished block will measure 12½" (31.5 cm) square (**Figure 7**).

8 Using template B, cut the concave piece from the orange/gray pieced block. Make a Drunkard's Path block using a burgundy template A piece and the orange/gray template B piece (**Figure 8**).

NOTE: *Refer to the illustration for the orientation of the orange/gray pieced block before using the template. See Curved Piecing in chapter 1 for tips on sewing smooth curves.*

9 In the same manner, use template B to cut a concave piece from the lavender/orange pieced block. Make a Drunkard's Path block using a burgundy template A piece and the lavender/orange template B piece (**Figure 9**).

NOTE: *Refer to the illustration for the orientation of the Lavender/Orange pieced block before using the template.*

10 Make 1 Drunkard's Path block using 1 aqua A piece and 1 lavender B piece.

11 Using 4 of the orange template B pieces, make the following Drunkard's Path blocks: 3 with burgundy template A pieces and 1 with a lavender template A piece.

12 For the last Drunkard's Path block, sew 5 lavender B strips to 5 orange B strips, alternating colors. Cut 1 using template A from this unit. Sew the striped A piece to the remaining orange template B piece (**Figure 10**).

NOTE: *Refer to the illustration for the orientation of the orange/lavender unit before using the template.*

13 Following **Figure 11**, sew the Drunkard's Path blocks to the pieced stripe blocks and the orange I rectangle.

TIP: *Pin at each stripe to keep the alignment accurate.*

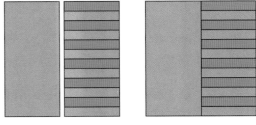

Fig. 7

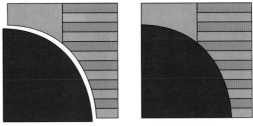

Fig. 8

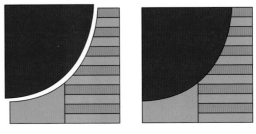

Fig. 9

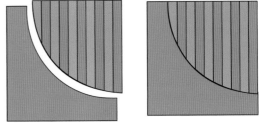

Fig. 10

ASSEMBLE SECTION C

Refer to **Figure 12** throughout section C assembly.

14 Sew 2 orange C strips to 1 lavender C strip, alternating colors.

15 Sew the lavender strip E to the left end of the orange/lavender stripe unit, the lavender F strip to the right, and the lavender J strip to the bottom of the unit.

16 Sew 11 orange C strips to 11 gray C strips, alternating colors.

17 Sew the gray H strip to the left side of the orange/gray strip unit (with the orange strip on top) and the gray K strip to the right side.

18 Sew 9 aqua D strips to 9 gray D strips, alternating colors.

19 Sew the units together as shown.

FINISHING

20 Arrange sections A, B, and C as shown in **Figure 13**.

21 Divide backing into (2) 1⅞ yard (1.7 m) lengths. Sew the pieces lengthwise.

22 Layer the backing, batting, and quilt top; baste. Quilt as desired. The quilt shown was quilted with a combination of straight lines and geometric textures.

23 Sew 2¼" (5.5 cm) binding strips into 1 continuous piece. Add binding to quilt (see French-Fold Binding in chapter 1 for directions).

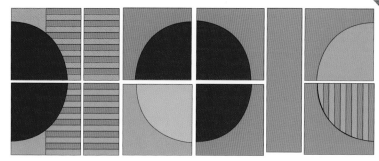

Fig. 11

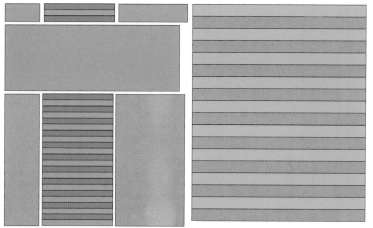

Fig. 12

Fig. 13

FINISHED SIZE

81" (206 cm) square

MATERIALS

*Fabric requirements assume 40"
(101.5 cm) usable width of fabric.*

White fabric for strips and
background, 7 yards (6.4 cm)

Blue fabric, 3 yards (2.7 m) or
(39) 2½" × 40" (6.5 cm × 101.5 cm)
precut strips for center motif
and binding

Backing fabric (108"-wide [274
cm]), 2½ yards (2.3 m) (white or
very light color recommended)

12"-wide (30.5 cm) iron-on
tearaway stabilizer, 9 yards (8.2 m)

Batting, queen-size

Cotton or non-stretch string,
1 yard (0.9 m)

Fabric-safe marker

*All seams are ¼" (6 mm) unless
otherwise indicated.*

RADIO QUILT

ROSEMARIE DEBOER
Quilted by TIA CURTIS

Inspired by the speaker from a 1950s radio,
this quilt uses precut strips to form a center
motif—created with the basic string-and-pencil
method for drawing a semicircle—and needle-
turn appliqué to get that perfect, rounded edge.
A technique for sewing long strips together
perfectly every time is included. It will add a
little time to the construction, but it's worth it!

CUTTING DIRECTIONS

Background panels are exact length needed. You may want to make them longer to allow for piecing variations.

FROM THE WHITE FABRIC, CUT:

(28) 2½" × 30" (6.5 cm × 76 cm) strips for the center motif

(3) 2½" × 40" (6.5 cm × 101.5 cm) strips for the vertical column

(2) 40" × 82" (101.5 cm × 208 cm) panels for background

FROM THE BLUE PRECUTS, CUT:

(30) 2½" × 30" (6.5 cm × 76 cm) strips for center motif

(9) 2½" × 40" (6.5 cm × 101.5 cm) strips for binding

CIRCLE ASSEMBLY

1   Sew a 30" (76 cm) blue strip to a 30" (76 cm) white strip lengthwise to make a blue/white set. Make 28 sets. (See the Keep Narrow Strips Straight sidebar for tips on preventing the strip sets from wobbling.)

2   Sew 14 pairs of blue/white sets together. Sew the remaining 30" (76 cm) blue strip to the white strip on the end. Make 2 blue/white rectangles of 15 blue strips alternated with 14 white strips.

3   Cut a 29" (73.5 cm) length of string. Wind and tape 1" (2.5 cm) of the string around a fabric-safe marker. Holding the other end of the string at the center of the middle blue strip, mark a semicircle on the top of the pieced rectangle (**Figure 1**). Mark both pieced rectangles.

     NOTE: *Mark carefully to get an accurate semicircle.*

4   Cut the semicircle on the marked line (**Figure 2**).

5   Center the semicircle on a background panel. Baste the straight edges together (**Figure 3**). Pin baste the blue/white semicircle to the background, measuring frequently to keep the lines straight.

6   Needle-turn appliqué the curved edge to the background. Make 2.

QUILT ASSEMBLY

7   Sew the (3) 2½" × 40" (6.5 cm × 101.5 cm) white strips together with diagonal seams to form 1 long strip. Cut a 2½" × 82" (6.5 cm × 208 cm) length for the center vertical column.

8   Referring to **Figure 4**, arrange the 2 appliquéd sections and the vertical column.

9   Sew the column between the sections.

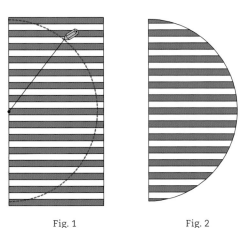

Fig. 1   Fig. 2

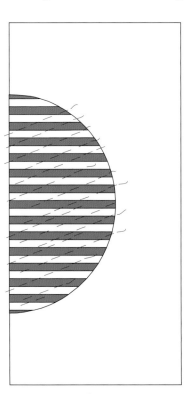

Fig. 3

FINISHING

10 Layer backing, batting, and quilt top; baste. Quilt as desired. Quilt shown here was quilted with horizontal matchstick quilting on the blue and white appliqué and vertical matchstick quilting on the background and center column.

11 Sew 2½"-wide (6.5 cm) binding strips into 1 continuous piece. Bind the quilt (see French-Fold Binding in chapter 1 for directions).

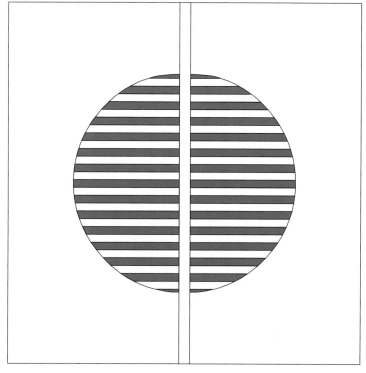

Fig. 4

Keep Narrow Strips Straight

If these long strips wobble, the crisp, modern look of this quilt will, well, not be so crisp and modern. The following technique will take some time at the outset, but will save you hours of grief and despair.

1   Cut (30) 2" × 30" (5 cm × 76 cm) lengths of stabilizer. If your stabilizer isn't that long, fuse strips together in step 3.

2   Perforate the stabilizer down the middle lengthwise. Use a serrated tracing wheel or stitch down the length with no thread in the needle. If you can retain the accuracy, stack a few strips and perforate them at the same time (**Figure A**).

3   Place the perforated strip, fusible side up, on an ironing board.

4   Align 1 white strip and 1 blue strip, right side up, on the fusible, with the cut edges meeting at the perforated line (**Figure B**).

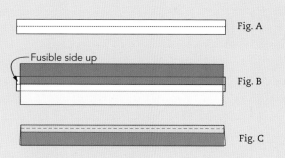

5   Press to adhere the fabric to the stabilizer.

6   Fold the stabilized strips with the stabilizer on the outside.

7   Stitch ¼" (6 mm) from the perforated edge (**Figure C**).

8   Tear away the stabilizer and press the seams toward the darker fabric.

FINISHED QUILT

66" × 86" (168 cm × 218 cm)

MATERIALS

Khaki fabric, ¾ yard (0.7 m)

Hot pink fabric, ⅝ yard (0.6 m)

Misty green fabric, ¼ yard (0.2 m)

Green cross print fabric, ¼ yard (0.2 m)

Cornflower blue fabric, ¼ yard (0.2 m)

Aqua fabric, ⅜ yard (0.3 m)

Coral fabric, ½ yard (0.5 m)

Deep blue fabric, ⅜ yard (0.3 m)

Salmon fabric, ½ yard (0.5 m)

Salmon cross print fabric, ½ yard (0.5 m)

Dark green fabric, ½ yard (0.5 m)

Mustard fabric, ⅝ yard (0.6 m)

Teal cross print fabric, ⅝ yard (0.6 m)

Mint fabric, ⅝ yard (0.6 m)

Purple fabric, ⅜ yard (0.3 m)

Backing fabric, 5½ yards (5 m)

Batting, full-size

Binding, ⅝ yard (0.6 m)

TIP: *Purchase the fabric off the bolt (instead of using fat quarters) to maximize the length of each strip.*

All seams are ¼" (6 mm) unless otherwise indicated.

MODERN COURTHOUSE QUILT

SIOBHAN ROGERS

Quilted by KIM BRADLEY

Illustrations by Siobhan Rogers

Siobhan loves the Log Cabin block and its innumerable variations, especially Courthouse Steps. This classically traditional block looks so fresh and modern as an entire quilt top in solids and subtle prints. Consider using curly and curved quilting to counterbalance the pure geometric quality of this setting.

CUTTING DIRECTIONS

Cut all of the strips at once, making sure to organize and label strips with the corresponding round number.

NOTE: *The colors Khaki and Hot pink are repeated in the quilt top.*

FROM KHAKI FABRIC, CUT:

(1) 2¼" (5.5 cm) × WOF (width-of-fabric) strips (round 1)

(8) 2½" (6.5 cm) × WOF strips (round 18)

FROM HOT PINK FABRIC, CUT:

(2) 1½" (3.8 cm) × WOF strips (round 2)

(5) 1½" (3.8 cm) × WOF strips (round 10)

(6) 1½" (3.8 cm) × WOF strips (round 14)

FROM MISTY GREEN FABRIC, CUT:

(2) 3¼" (8.5 cm) × WOF strips (round 3)

FROM GREEN CROSS PRINT, CUT:

(2) 2½" (6.5 cm) × WOF strips (round 4)

FROM CORNFLOWER BLUE FABRIC, CUT:

(3) 2" (5 cm) × WOF strips (round 5)

FROM AQUA FABRIC, CUT:

(3) 2¾" (7 cm) × WOF strips (round 6)

FROM CORAL FABRIC, CUT:

(4) 3¾" (9.5 cm) × WOF strips (round 7)

FROM DEEP BLUE FABRIC, CUT:

(4) 2½" (6.5 cm) × WOF strips (round 8)

FROM SALMON FABRIC, CUT:

(5) 2½" (6.5 cm) × WOF strips (round 9)

FROM SALMON CROSS PRINT FABRIC, CUT:

(5) 2½" (6.5 cm) × WOF strips (round 11)

FROM GREEN DARK FABRIC, CUT:

(6) 2¼" (5.5 cm) × WOF strips (round 12)

FROM MUSTARD FABRIC, CUT:

(6) 3" (7.5 cm) × WOF strips (round 13)

FROM TEAL CROSS PRINT FABRIC, CUT:

(7) 2½" (6.5 cm) × WOF strips (round 15)

FROM MINT FABRIC, CUT:

(7) 2¾" (7 cm) × WOF strips (round 16)

FROM PURPLE FABRIC, CUT:

(7) 1½" (3.8 cm) × WOF strips (round 17)

ASSEMBLE THE QUILT TOP

NOTE: *Press all seams toward the darker fabric.*

1 For the center, cut a 22" (56 cm) length from the round 1 strip.

2 Add the top and bottom strips (round 2) to the center strip. Press. Add the strips to the left and right side of the center strip. Press.

3 Continue adding strips in this order—top and bottom strips, then left and right side strips. Refer to **Figure 1**. Continue adding strips, ending with round 18 (khaki fabric). Press after each set of strips.

TIP: *Measure the quilt top after each round. If it is off-square, press to shape. (See the Tips for a Successful Courthouse Steps Quilt sidebar.)*

FINISH THE QUILT

4 Trim the selvedges from the backing fabric. Cut the yardage in half and sew the 2 pieces together along the long edge. Press the seam open.

5 Layer the backing wrong side up, followed by the batting, and then the quilt top, right side up. Baste the layers together using your preferred method.

6 Quilt as desired.

7 To make binding, cut (8) 2¼" (5.5 cm) × WOF strips from the binding fabric. Remove the selvedges from the binding strips and sew them together with a diagonal seam, trimming and pressing these seams open, to create 1 long strip. Fold the binding in half, wrong sides together, along the entire length of the strip. Press. Attach the binding using your preferred method. (See French-Fold Binding in chapter 1 for directions.)

Tips for a Successful Courthouse Steps Quilt

- To stay organized, label the WOF strips by round number after they are cut and before cutting the next color.

- Sew all of the cut strips for each round into 1 long strip before adding it to the quilt. By working with a longer strip, the joining seams will occur randomly and be less obvious.

- Measure and cut equal-length strips before sewing them to the previous round. For example, the left and right side lengths should be the same measurement. This keeps the quilt squared up so it will lie flat when complete.

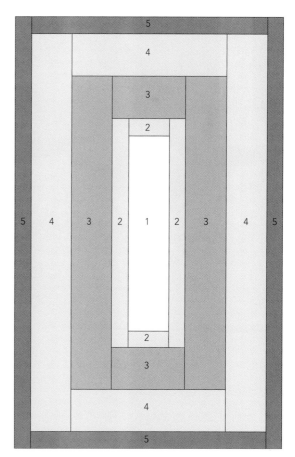

Fig. 1

FINISHED SIZE

63" (160 cm) square

FINISHED BLOCK SIZE

9" (23 cm) square

MATERIALS

Fabric requirements assume 40" (101.5 cm) usable width of fabric.

Orange fabric, ⅜ yard (0.3 m)

Aqua fabric, 1½ yards (1.4 m)

White background fabric, 3½ yards (3.2 m)

Backing, 4 yards (3.6 m)

Binding, ½ yard (0.5 m)

Batting, twin-size

Fabric-safe marker

All seams are ¼" (6 mm) unless otherwise indicated.

ISLANDS IN THE STREAM QUILT

PAMELA COBB
Quilted by LYNN RINEHART

Like a perfect duet, this two-block quilt takes advantage of easy piecing to create dramatic movement between the islands along the virtual stream. Keeping it simple with a mix of techniques from strip piecing to sew-and-flip blocks, the asymmetric layout adds interest without complexity.

CUTTING DIRECTIONS

Measurements include ¼" (6 mm) seam allowances. Label the blocks as you cut. Press seams open unless otherwise noted.

FROM ORANGE FABRIC, CUT:

(3) 3½" × 40" (9 cm × 101.5 cm) strips

FROM AQUA FABRIC, CUT:

(5) 6½" × 40" (16.5 cm × 101.5 cm) strips; subcut (36) 5" × 6½" (12.5 cm × 16.5 cm) A rectangles for the Stream blocks

(3) 3½" × 40" (9 cm × 101.5 cm) strips; subcut (33) 3½" (9 cm) B squares for the Island blocks

FROM WHITE FABRIC, CUT:

For the Stream blocks:

(2) 2" × 40" (5 cm × 101.5 cm) strips; subcut (36) 2" (5 cm) C squares

(4) 3½" × 40" (9 cm × 101.5 cm) strips; subcut (36) 3½" (9 cm) D squares

(2) 9½" × 40" (24 cm × 101.5 cm) strips; subcut (18) 3½" × 9½" (9 cm × 24 cm) E rectangles

For the Island blocks:

(3) 2½" × 40" (6.5 cm × 101.5 cm) strips

(3) 4½" × 40" (11.5 cm × 101.5 cm) strips

(6) 9½" × 40" (24 cm × 101.5 cm) strips.

From 2 strips, subcut (31) 2½" × 9½" (6.5 cm × 24 cm) F rectangles.

From the remaining strips, cut (31) 4½" × 9½" (11.5 cm × 24 cm) G rectangles.

FROM BINDING FABRIC, CUT:

(7) 2¼" × 40" (5.5 cm × 101.5 cm) strips

STREAM BLOCK ASSEMBLY

1 Mark a diagonal line on the backs of the 36 C squares and 36 D squares.

2 To make the Right Stream units (refer to **Figure 1**):

   a Place 1 marked D square on the bottom right corner of an A aqua rectangle. Sew just to the outside of the marked line. Trim the seam allowance to ¼" (6 mm) and press to the white fabric.

   b Place a marked C square on the top left corner of the A rectangle. Sew just to the outside of the marked line. Trim the seam allowance and press to the white. Make 18 Right Stream units.

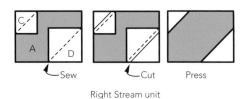

Right Stream unit

Fig. 1

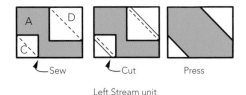

Left Stream unit

Fig. 2

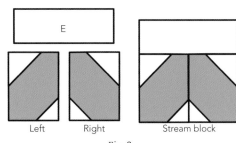

Fig. 3

3 To make the Left Stream units (Refer to **Figure 2**):

    a Place a marked D square on the top right corner of an A aqua rectangle. Sew just to the outside of the marked line. Trim the seam allowance and press to the white.

    b Place a marked C square on the bottom left corner of the A rectangle. Sew just to the outside of the marked line. Trim the seam allowance and press to the white. Make 18 Left Stream units.

4 Sew a Left Stream unit to a Right Stream unit and press the seam open. Sew an E rectangle to the top and press toward E. The block should measure 9½" (24 cm) square (**Figure 3**). Make 18 Stream blocks.

ISLAND BLOCK ASSEMBLY

5 Sew (1) 4½" × 40" (11.5 cm × 101.5 cm) white strip and (1) 2½" × 40" (6.5 cm × 101.5 cm) white strip to the sides of a 3½" × 40" (9 cm × 101.5 cm) orange strip to create a strip set. Make 3 strip sets measuring 9½" × 40" (24 cm × 101.5 cm).

6 From the strip sets, cut (31) 3½" × 9½" (9 cm × 24 cm) strip units (**Figure 4**).

7 Arrange 1 strip unit with the 2½" (6.5 cm) white piece at the top with an F rectangle on the right and a G rectangle to the left. Sew and press toward F and G. The block should measure 9½" (24 cm) square (**Figure 5**). Make 31 Island blocks.

8 For Island 1 blocks: Set aside 14 blocks.

9 For Island 2 blocks:

    a Mark a diagonal line on the backs of the 33 aqua B squares.

    b With a remaining Island block, position it so the orange square is offset to the top left. Place the B square on the lower right corner and sew just outside of the marked line. Trim seam allowance. Press to the aqua fabric.

    c Make 17. Label 6 of these blocks Island 2. The rest will be used to make Island 3 and Island 4 blocks.

10 For Island 3 blocks:

    a On the 11 remaining Island 2 blocks, position each block so the orange square is offset to the top left and an aqua triangle is in the bottom right. Place an aqua B square on the upper right corner and sew just outside of the marked line. Trim seam allowance. Press to the aqua fabric.

    b Make 11 blocks. Label 4 of these blocks Island 3. The rest will be used to make Island 4 blocks.

11 For Island 4 blocks:

    a On the 7 remaining Island 3 blocks, position each block so the orange square is offset to the top left and aqua triangles are in the top and bottom right. Place an aqua B square on the lower left corner and sew just outside of the marked line. Trim seam allowance. Press to the aqua fabric (**Figure 6**).

    b Make and label 7 Island 4 blocks.

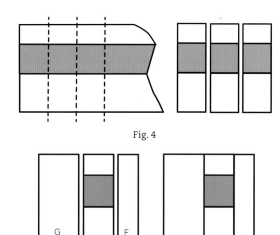

Fig. 4

Fig. 5

Island block

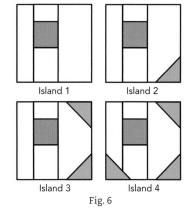

Island 1   Island 2

Island 3   Island 4

Fig. 6

QUILT TOP ASSEMBLY

12 Following **Figure 7**, arrange the blocks, paying careful attention to the orientation of the Stream and Island blocks.

13 Sew the blocks into rows. Sew the rows together to complete the quilt top.

TIP: *Use a pin to ensure the white and aqua seams match when sewing the blocks together.*

FINISHING

14 Divide the backing into (2) 2-yard (1.8 m) lengths. Sew panels lengthwise.

15 Layer backing, batting, and quilt top; baste. Quilt as desired. Quilt shown was quilted in the aqua "stream" with overlapping wavy lines to represent water flowing and an all-over pattern in the background and islands.

16 Sew the 2¼"-wide (5.5 cm) binding strips into 1 continuous piece (see French-Fold Binding in chapter 1 for directions). Bind the quilt.

Fig. 7

FINISHED SIZE

40" (101.5 cm) square

FINISHED BLOCK SIZE

4" (10 cm) square

MATERIALS

Charm pack of precut 5" (12.5 cm) squares

Background fabric, 1⅜ yards (1.3 m)

Backing fabric, 1¾ yards (1.6 m)

Binding, ½ yard (0.5 m)

Batting, 46" (117 cm) square (or a baby quilt size)

Fabric-safe marker

Rotary cutting supplies

All seams are ¼" (6 mm) unless otherwise indicated.

TWINKLE STAR QUILT

DEBBIE GRIFKA

Star quilts are timeless! To make this one modern, Debbie made one big star instead of several smaller ones, and used a charm pack of 5" (12.5 cm) squares to save some cutting time. The soft-colored fabrics from Sweetwater's "Hometown" fabric collection for Moda are beautiful, and this quilt would also be appealing in some vivid holiday or child-themed prints.

CUTTING DIRECTIONS

FROM BACKGROUND FABRIC, CUT:

(6) 4½" (11.5 cm) × WOF (width-of-fabric) strips; subcut 2 of the 4½" strips into (16) 4½" (11.5 cm) squares

NOTE: *Set aside the remaining (4) 4½" (11.5 cm) strips for the border.*

(2) 5" (12.5 cm) × WOF strips; subcut into (16) 5" (12.5 cm) squares

FROM BINDING FABRIC, CUT:

(5) 2½" (6.5 cm) × WOF strips

ASSEMBLING THE QUILT

1   Choose 16 dark and 16 medium fabrics from the charm pack. Save the rest for the quilt back or another project.

   TIP: *When selecting the medium and dark squares from your charm pack, avoid fabrics that blend too much with the background fabric.*

2   Start with 8 medium squares and 8 dark squares from the groups of 16; save the rest for step 8. On the wrong side of the 8 medium squares, draw a line from corner to corner, diagonally across the square (**Figure 1**).

3   Place a medium square on a dark square, right sides together.

4   Sew ¼" (6 mm) from the drawn line on each side of the line.

5   Cut along the line. Press the 2 pieced squares open, pressing the seams toward the darker fabrics. Trim the blocks to 4½" (11.5 cm) square.

6   Repeat this process with the remaining squares from the 2 groups of 8 to make a total of 16 Half-Square Triangle blocks. Trim the blocks to 4½" (11.5 cm) square.

7   On the wrong side of each of the (16) 5" (12.5 cm) background squares, draw a diagonal line from corner to corner.

8   Pair each of the remaining 8 medium and 8 dark squares with a background square and repeat steps 4–5 to make an additional 32 Half-Square Triangle blocks. Trim the blocks to 4½" (11.5 cm) square.

9   Using all 48 Half-Square Triangle blocks and (16) 4½" (11.5 cm) background squares, lay out the quilt according to **Figure** 2.

   NOTE: *Pay special attention to the positions of the dark and medium triangles.*

10 Sew the blocks into rows, and sew the rows together to make the quilt center.

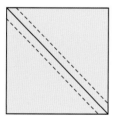

Fig. 1

Fig. 2

BORDER AND BINDING

11 Trim 2 of the border strips to 32½" (82.5 cm) and sew them to opposite sides of the quilt. Press the seams toward the border strips.

12 Trim the remaining 2 border strips to 40½" (103 cm). Sew them to the top and bottom of the quilt, and press.

13 Layer the quilt top with the backing and batting.

14 Quilt as desired. The quilt shown here was echo quilted inside the star. The background areas were quilted with horizontal, vertical, and diagonal lines to symbolize light radiating from the center of the star.

15 Join the binding strips together and bind the edges of the quilt as desired. (See French-Fold Binding in chapter 1 for directions.)

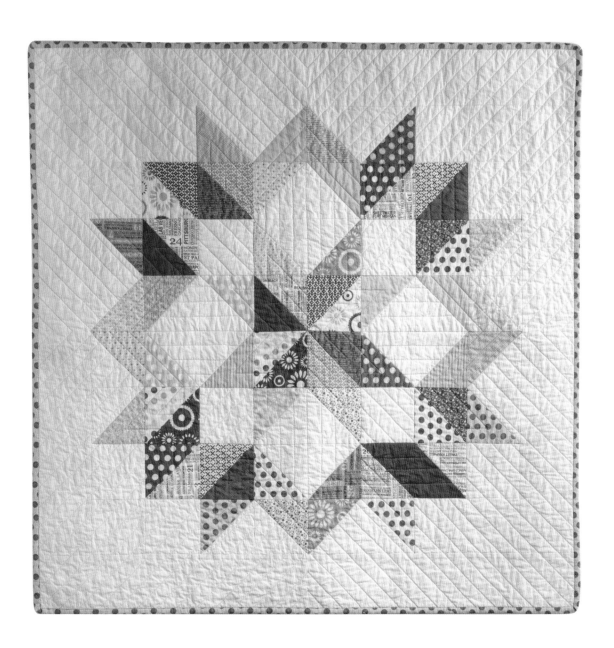

FINISHED QUILT SIZE

48½" × 64½" (123 cm × 164 cm)

FINISHED BLOCK

4" × 8" (10 cm × 20.5 cm)

MATERIALS

Light and dark fabrics, 36 assorted fat quarters (each 18" × 21" [45.5 cm × 53.5 cm]) for the quilt top (We used 18 light and 18 dark fabrics)

Binding, ½ yard (0.5 m)

Backing, 3 yards (2.7 m)

Batting, twin-size

Paper-piecing patterns (see Templates section)

Cutting templates 2 and 3 (see Templates section)

Cardstock

OPTIONAL

Glue stick, washable

Acrylic ruler

All seams are ¼" (6 mm) unless otherwise indicated.

FLIGHT DELIGHT QUILT

VIVIKA HANSEN DENEGRE

Quilted by SAIMA DAVIS

Made by THE MODERN PATCHWORK EDITORIAL AND DESIGN TEAMS

Do you love the winged birds, butterflies, and bees of springtime? A fat quarter bundle of playful bright polka dots, dreamy pinstripes, and neutral prints from Dear Stella's Intermix collection is all you need to create this charming quilt.

CUTTING DIRECTIONS

Separate the fabric into 18 lights and 18 darks. The dark fabrics will be the main color fabric (1), and the lighter fabrics will be used for the background pieces (2 and 3).

FROM THE DARK FABRICS, CUT:

(96) 5" × 9" (12.5 cm × 23 cm) rectangles

FROM THE LIGHT FABRICS, CUT:

48 triangles using template 2

48 using template 2Rev

48 triangles using template 3

48 using template 3Rev

FROM THE BINDING FABRIC, CUT:

(8) 2¼" (5.5 cm) × WOF (width-of-fabric) strips

PAPER PIECE THE BLOCKS

Refer to **Figure 1** while piecing the blocks.

1 Make 48 copies each of paper-piecing patterns A and ARev. Check copies for accuracy.

2 Place a 5" × 9" (12.5 cm × 23 cm) colored rectangle on the unprinted side of a paper-piecing pattern with the wrong side of the fabric against the paper. Pin in place, or secure with a small amount of glue from a glue stick.

3 Turn the pattern printed-side up. Place the sheet of cardstock along the diagonal seam line between piece 1 and 2. Fold the paper back to reveal the fabric. Using an acrylic ruler and rotary cutter, trim the fabric to create a ¼" (6 mm) seam allowance. Repeat on the diagonal line between piece 1 and 3.

4 Sew pieces 2 and 3 in place using your favorite paper-piecing method.

NOTE: *Press after sewing each seam to make sure the new piece entirely covers the paper. Leave the paper in place until after the blocks are trimmed. Make 48 A blocks and 48 ARev blocks.*

5 Trim each block to 4½" × 8½" (11.5 cm × 21.5 cm) and remove the paper. Press.

Tips for paper piecing

• When paper piecing, the fabric is sewn directly on a piece of paper on which the pattern has been printed. You will need one paper pattern for each block.

• Check that the printed patterns are accurate. Sometimes printers and scanners slightly change dimensions; make sure the printed pattern is the same size as the original.

• Cut the fabric a bit generously. Although it feels wasteful, it will save time and fabric in the long run.

• Shorten your stitch length to 1.8 mm to make it easier to remove the paper.

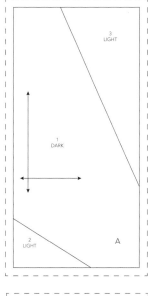

Fig. 1

Fig. 2

ASSEMBLE THE QUILT TOP

6 Following **Figure 2**, arrange the blocks on a design wall. Rotating the blocks in alternating rows creates the "butterfly" effect.

7 Sew the blocks into rows. Sew the rows together.

FINISH THE QUILT

8 Trim the selvedges from the backing fabric. Cut the fabric length in half and sew it together along the long edge, creating a large rectangle. Press the seam open.

9 Make the quilt sandwich by placing the backing wrong side up, followed by the batting, and then the quilt top, right side up. Baste.

10 Quilt as desired.

11 Join the 2¼" (5.5 cm) binding strips with diagonal seams to create a straight-grain binding strip. Fold the strip in half lengthwise and bind the quilt (see French-Fold Binding in chapter 1 for directions).

FINISHED SIZE

54½" (138.5 cm) square

FINISHED BLOCK SIZE

4½" (11.5 cm) square

MATERIALS

Black fabric,1¼ yards (1.1 m) or
(60) 5" (12.5 cm) squares

White fabric, 1¾ yards (1.6 m) or
(84) 5" (12.5 cm) precut squares

Backing, 3¼ yards (3 m)

Binding, ½ yard (0.5 m)

Batting, 60" (152.5 cm) square

*All seams are ¼" (6 mm) unless
otherwise indicated.*

GRAPHIC CROSS QUILT

ALLIE HEATH

This simple yet striking quilt combines the bold contrast of solid black and white fabrics in a graphic repeating pattern. Made with precut squares, stitching up this quilt couldn't be easier—or more fun!

CUTTING DIRECTIONS

FROM BLACK FABRIC, CUT:

(60) 5" (12.5 cm) squares

FROM WHITE FABRIC, CUT:

(60) 5" (12.5 cm) squares

MAKE THE BLOCKS

1   Stitch the squares together to make the Nine Patch blocks (**Figures 1-3**).

2   Following **Figure 4**, stitch the blocks into rows as shown.

3   Sew the rows together, carefully matching the seams.

ASSEMBLE THE QUILT

4   Trim the selvedges from the backing fabric. Cut the yardage in half.

5   Piece the backing with one vertical seam. Press the seam open. Trim the backing to 4" (10 cm) larger than the quilt top.

6   Layer the backing wrong side up, followed by the batting, and then the quilt top, right side up.

7   Baste the layers together using the method of your choice.

8   Quilt as desired. The quilt shown here was quilted with straight lines and graphic squares with black thread on the black fabric and white on the white fabric.

9   Cut and piece (6) 2¼" (5.5 cm) × WOF (width-of-fabric) strips from the binding fabric. Join the strips together to create 1 long strip.

10 Bind the quilt as desired. (See French-Fold Binding in chapter 1 for directions.)

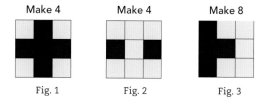

Make 4   Make 4   Make 8

Fig. 1   Fig. 2   Fig. 3

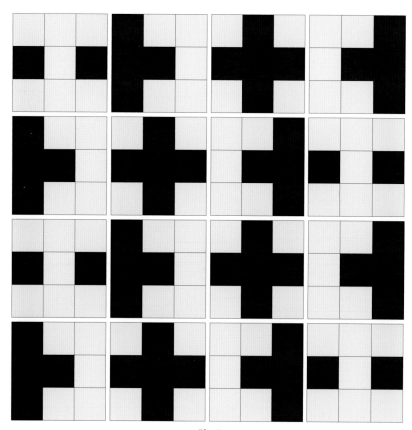

Fig. 4

FINISHED SIZE

51" × 64" (129.5 cm × 162.5 cm)

FINISHED BLOCK SIZE

12¾" (32.5 cm) square

MATERIALS

Solid color fabric, (10) ¾ yards
(0.7 m) each

Coordinating prints (with solids),
2 fat quarters (each 18" × 21"
[45.5 cm × 53.5 cm])

Light striped fabric, ½ yard (0.5 m)

Backing fabric, 3¼ yards (3 m)

Binding fabric, ½ yard (0.5 m)

Batting, twin-size

Template plastic or cardboard

Hot Cross Buns Templates
(see Templates section)

*All seams are ¼" (6 mm) unless
otherwise indicated.*

HOT CROSS BUNS QUILT

ANNMARIE COWLEY

Whimsical striped strips are suspended in bold-colored circles to create a variation on the traditional Drunkard's Path block. For a bit of the unexpected, coordinating prints are substituted in a few places throughout the quilt.

CUTTING DIRECTIONS

Measurements include ¼" (6 mm) seam allowances. Trace each template onto template material. Cut out and label the templates. See **Figure 1** for nesting templates for the most efficient use of fabric. Label pieces as you cut. Press seams open.

FROM EACH SOLID, CUT:

(2) 7" × 40" (18 cm × 101.5 cm) strips. From the strips, cut 8 template A.

(1) 7½" × 40" (19 cm × 101.5 cm) strip. From the strip, cut 8 template B (there will be extras).

(1) 1¼" × 40" (3.2 cm × 101.5 cm) strip. From the strip, cut: (2) 1¼" (3.2 cm) C squares, (8) 1" × 1¼" (2.5 cm × 3.2 cm) D rectangles, and (8) 1¼" × 2½" (3.2 cm × 6.5 cm) E rectangles.

FROM PRINT FAT QUARTERS, CUT:

5 template B

FROM STRIPE FABRIC, CUT:

(3) 4½" × 40" (11.5 cm × 101.5 cm) strips. From the strips, cut (80) 1¼" × 4½" (3.2 cm × 11.5 cm) F rectangles.

FROM BINDING FABRIC, CUT:

(7) 2¼" × 40" (5.5 × 101.5) strips

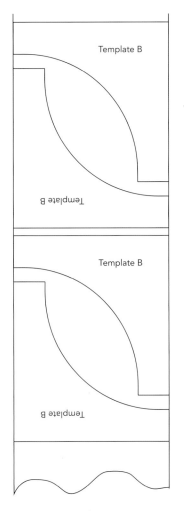

Fig. 1

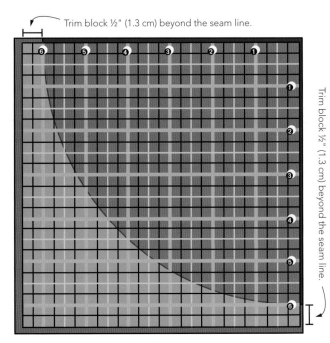

Trim block ½" (1.3 cm) beyond the seam line.

Trim block ½" (1.3 cm) beyond the seam line.

Fig. 2

ASSEMBLE THE QUILT

1   Using the template A and template B pieces, arrange 20 blocks on a design wall in 5 rows with 4 blocks each (refer to **Figure 4** for help arranging the blocks).

    NOTE: *Substitute a print template B for a solid in 5 color groupings.*

2   Referring to Curved Piecing in chapter 1, sew template A to template B. Make 80 A/B units.

3   Referring to **Figure 2**, trim all of the units to 6½" (16.5 cm) square, leaving ½" (1.3 cm) of background (template B fabric) past the center quarter circle (template A fabric). Group all A/B units by color in 20 sets of 4.

4   Working with 1 A/B color set at a time and following **Figure 3**, arrange 4 striped F rectangles, 4 E rectangles matching the A color, 4 D rectangles, and 1 C square matching the B color.

5   Sew together D, E, and F rectangles. Make 4.

6   Sew a D/E/F unit to either side of a C square to create a center sashing strip.

7   Sew an A/B unit to either side of a D/E/F unit. Make 2 units.

8   Sew the A/B/D/E/F units to either side of the center sashing strip to complete the block. Make 20 blocks.

9   Referring to **Figure 4**, arrange the blocks on a design wall.

10 Sew the blocks into rows; sew the rows to complete the quilt top.

FINISH THE QUILT

11 Divide the backing into (2) 1⅝-yard (1.5 m) lengths. Sew panels lengthwise.

12 Layer backing, batting, and quilt top; baste. Quilt as desired. Quilt shown here was quilted with "seersucker" quilting (3 matchstick lines, skip a line, repeat).

13 Sew 2¼"-wide (5.5 cm) binding strips into 1 continuous piece for a straight-grain French-fold binding (see French-Fold Binding in chapter 1 for directions.)

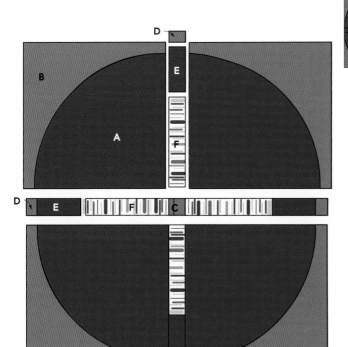

Fig. 3

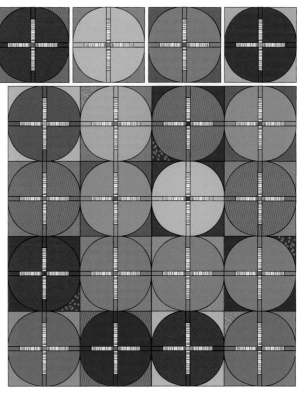

Fig.4

FINISHED SIZE

72" (183 cm) square

FINISHED BLOCK SIZE

12" (30.5 cm) square

MATERIALS

Solid fabrics, 36 fat quarters (each
18" × 21" [45.5 cm × 53.5 cm]) in
different colors for the petals

Coordinating prints, (2) 4" (10 cm)
squares each in 36 different colors

White background fabric, 4½ yards
(4.1 cm)

Backing, 4½ yards (4.1 m)

Binding, ⅝ yards (0.6 m)

Batting, 76" (193 cm) square

Template plastic or cardboard

Conservatory Gardens Quilt
templates (see Templates section)

OPTIONAL

Acrylic ruler, 3½" (9 cm) square

Rotary cutter and mat

*All seams are ¼" (6 mm) unless
otherwise indicated.*

CONSERVATORY GARDENS QUILT

JEN CARLTON-BAILLY

Illustrations by Jen Carlton-Bailly

Inspired by all the glorious cotton solids, create
a garden using fat quarter bundles that will
make you want stop and smell the flowers. This
pattern combines simple curves to create perfect
blooms for your personal garden.

CUTTING DIRECTIONS

Trace templates A and B onto the template material and cut out. Organize cut-out fabric pieces for each template by color.

FROM EACH COLOR FAT QUARTER, CUT:

14 pieces using template A (total 504 pieces)

FROM COORDINATING PRINTS, CUT:

72 pieces using template A

FROM BACKGROUND FABRIC, CUT:

(36) 4" (10 cm) x WOF (width-of-fabric) strips; subcut 576 pieces using template B (each strip yields 16 pieces)

NOTE: *Nest the pieces for the most efficient use of fabric* (**Figure 1**).

MAKE THE BLOCKS

Refer to **Figure 2** for steps 1–3.

1   Sew a template B piece to each template A piece. Press seam allowances toward A. (See Curved Piecing in chapter 1 for tips.)

2   Form each flower by arranging the 14 solid color petals with 2 coordinating prints.

NOTE: *Placing the prints randomly gives the quilt energy.*

3   Sew the units into rows. Sew the rows together to form the block. Make 36 blocks.

ARRANGE THE BLOCKS

4   Once all flower blocks are sewn, follow **Figure 3** to place the blocks. Match the seams. Press seams open to achieve a flat block (**Figure 4**).

NOTE: *The placement of coordinating scraps should be random. Rotate the block if two patterns happen to be next to each other.*

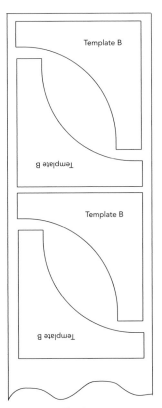

Fig. 1

Tips for Success

• Cut up to 4 layers of fabric at a time—but no more, as the fabric will shift.

• Start with a new blade in your rotary cutter.

• Batching tasks helps establish a more efficient routine when sewing. Cut all the pieces first, then move to pinning, sewing, pressing, and finally squaring them all up.

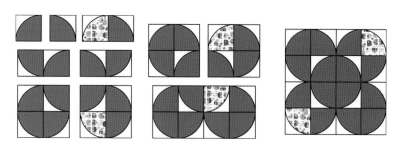

Fig. 2

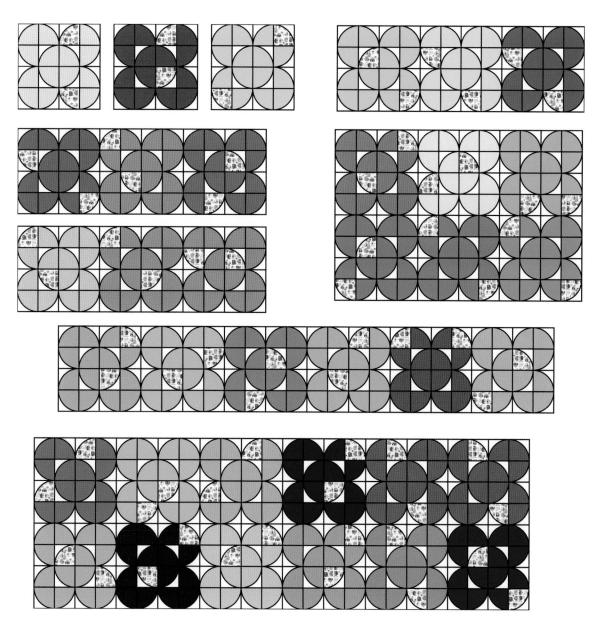

Fig. 3

Fig. 4

FINISH THE QUILT

5 Trim the selvedges from the backing fabric. Cut the fabric length in half and sew it together along the long edge, creating a large rectangle. Press the seam open.

6 Make the quilt sandwich by placing the backing wrong side up, followed by the batting, and then the quilt top, right side up. Baste.

7 Quilt as desired. The quilt shown here was quilted using a slight curve starting at the top right corner and moving outwards.

8 Bind your quilt as desired. (See French-Fold Binding in chapter 1 for directions.)

Templates

Unless otherwise noted, copy all templates at 100% with no scaling. Double check that your patterns are the appropriate size by measuring the box on each page. It should measure 1" (2.5cm). For templates that are larger than 8" × 10½" (20.5 × 26.5 cm), the patterns are divided into multiple pieces. You will need to copy them on separate pages and tape them together at the registration marks. F+W Media grants permission to photocopy these templates for personal use only.

PENCIL HOLDER
MAKE 4 COPIES OF THIS PAGE TO CREATE 8 TEMPLATES.

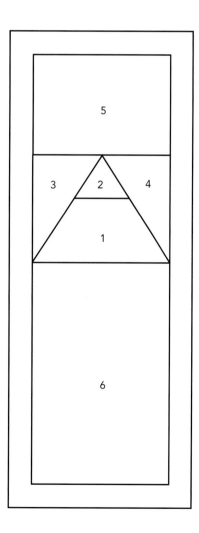
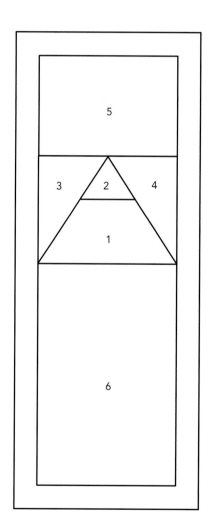

This square should measure 1" (2.5 cm) square when copied.

MAKE 2 COPIES OF THIS PAGE TO CREATE 20 HEXAGONS.
YOU WILL HAVE 1 EXTRA HEXAGON.

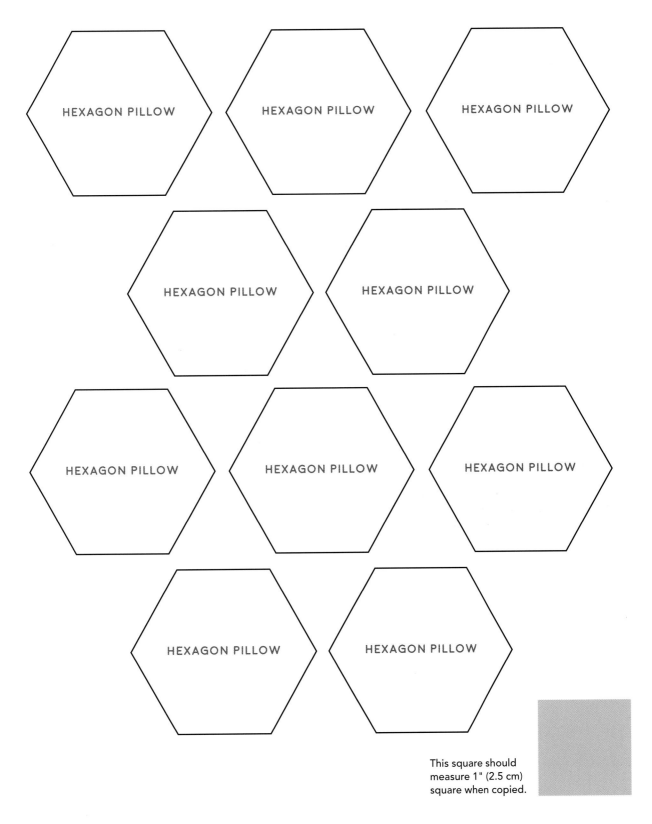

HEXAGON PILLOW

HEXAGON PILLOW

HEXAGON PILLOW

HEXAGON PILLOW

HEXAGON PILLOW

HEXAGON PILLOW

HEXAGON PILLOW

HEXAGON PILLOW

HEXAGON PILLOW

HEXAGON PILLOW

This square should
measure 1" (2.5 cm)
square when copied.

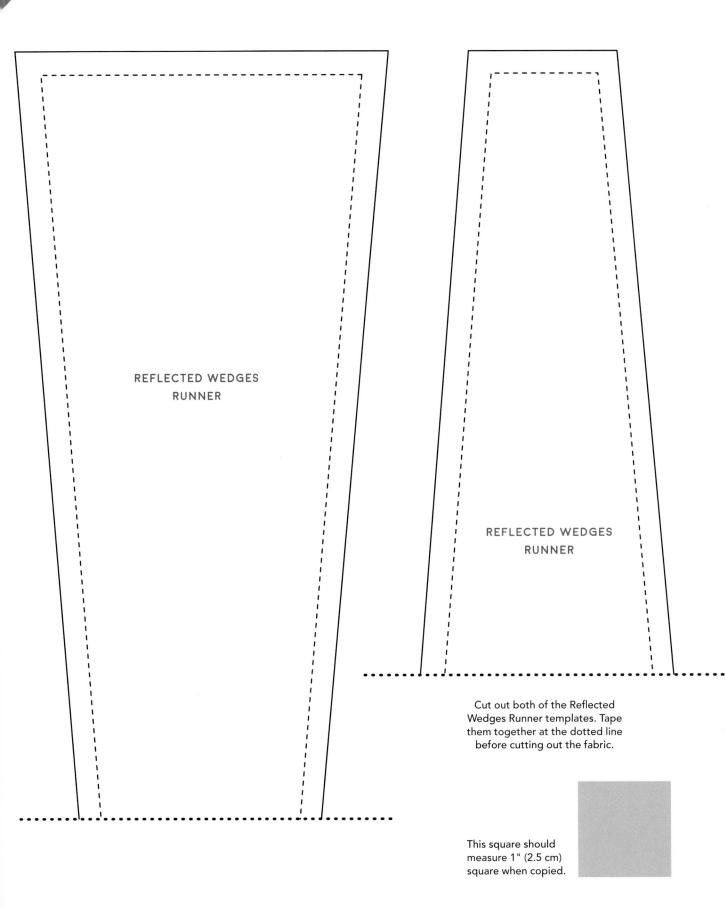

REFLECTED WEDGES
RUNNER

REFLECTED WEDGES
RUNNER

Cut out both of the Reflected
Wedges Runner templates. Tape
them together at the dotted line
before cutting out the fabric.

This square should
measure 1" (2.5 cm)
square when copied.

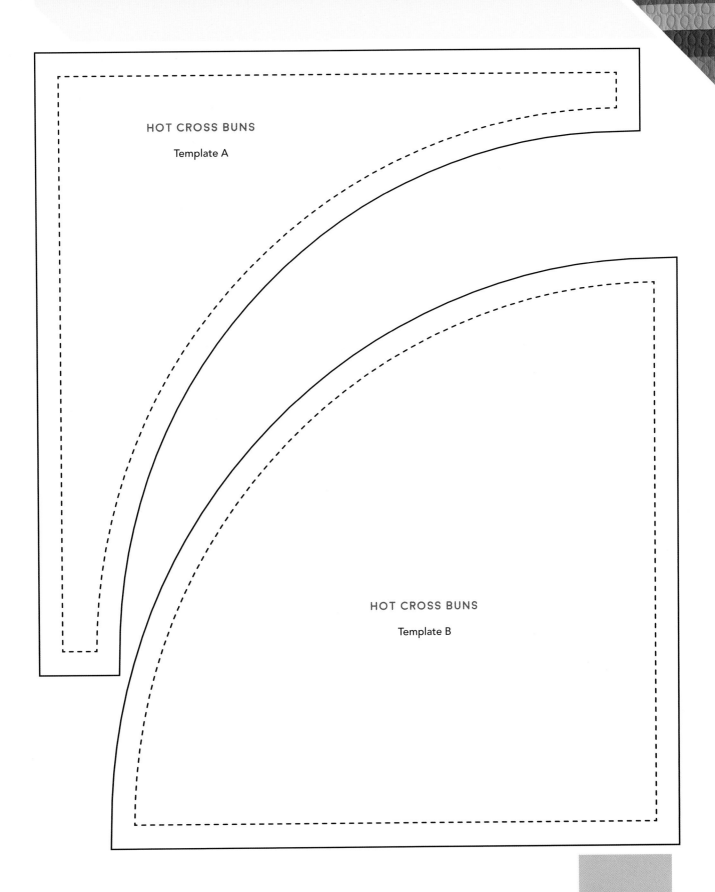

HOT CROSS BUNS

Template A

HOT CROSS BUNS

Template B

This square should measure 1" (2.5 cm) square when copied.

THIS TEMPLATE NEEDS TO BE ENLARGED TO 140%
FOR THE SQUARE AT THE BOTTOM OF THE PAGE
TO MEASURE 1" (2.5CM).

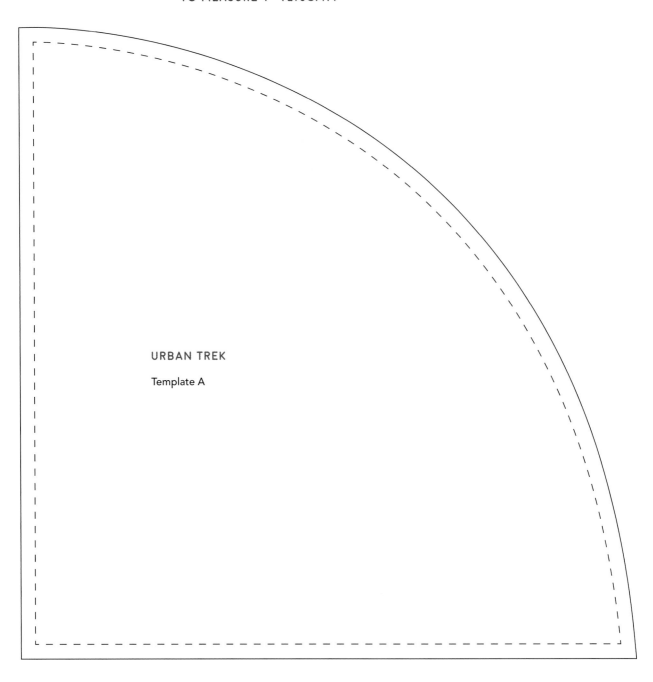

URBAN TREK

Template A

This square should
measure 1" (2.5 cm)
square when copied.

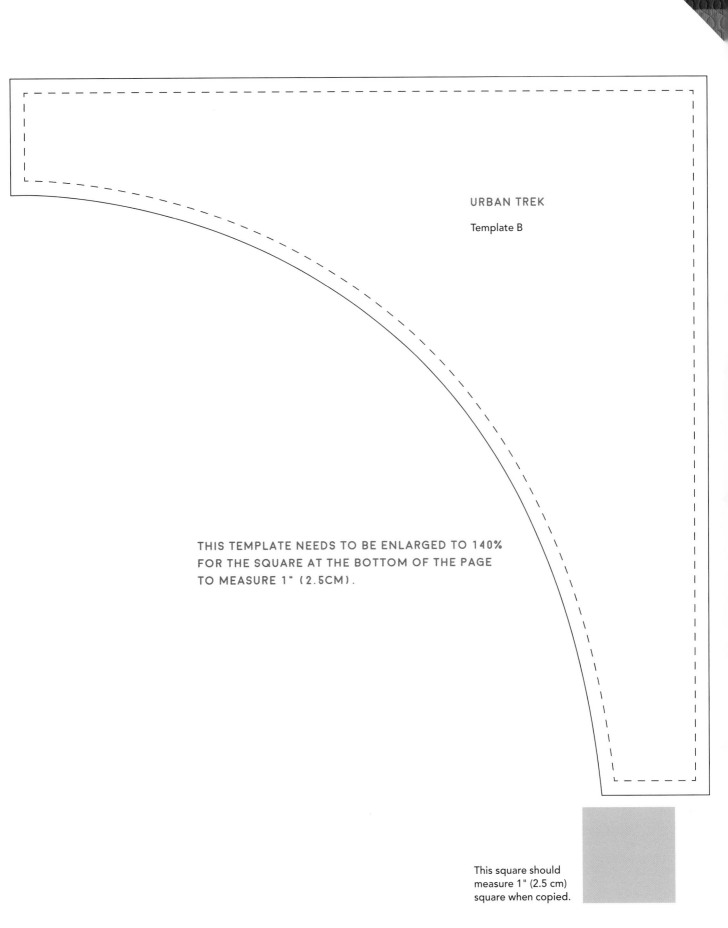

URBAN TREK

Template B

THIS TEMPLATE NEEDS TO BE ENLARGED TO 140%
FOR THE SQUARE AT THE BOTTOM OF THE PAGE
TO MEASURE 1" (2.5CM).

This square should
measure 1" (2.5 cm)
square when copied.

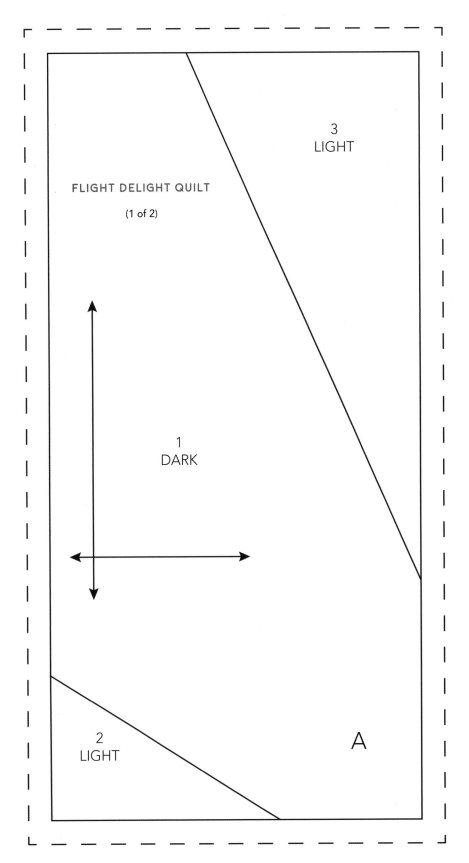

FLIGHT DELIGHT QUILT

(1 of 2)

3
LIGHT

1
DARK

2
LIGHT

A

This square should measure 1" (2.5 cm) square when copied.

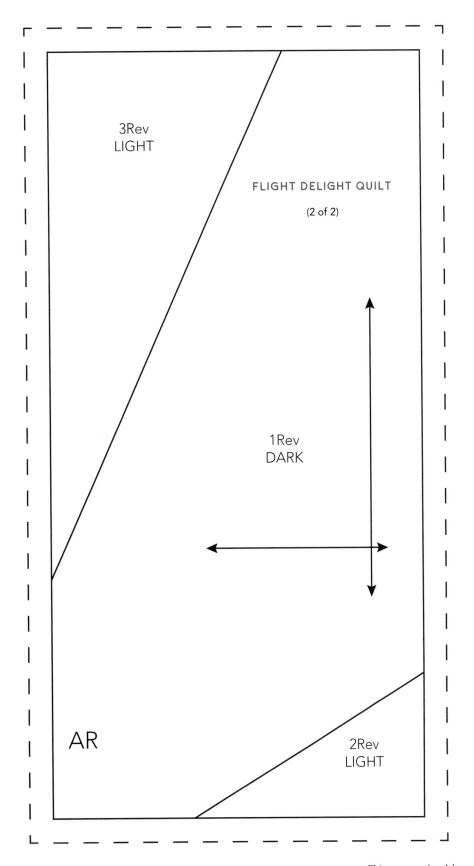

3Rev
LIGHT

FLIGHT DELIGHT QUILT

(2 of 2)

1Rev
DARK

AR

2Rev
LIGHT

This square should
measure 1" (2.5 cm)
square when copied.

THIS TEMPLATE IS FOR THE QUILTED PATCHWORK APRON AND THE
CONSERVATORY GARDENS QUILT.

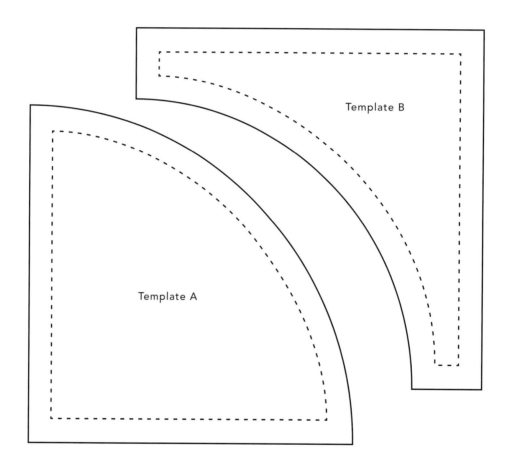

Template B

Template A

This square should
measure 1" (2.5 cm)
square when copied.

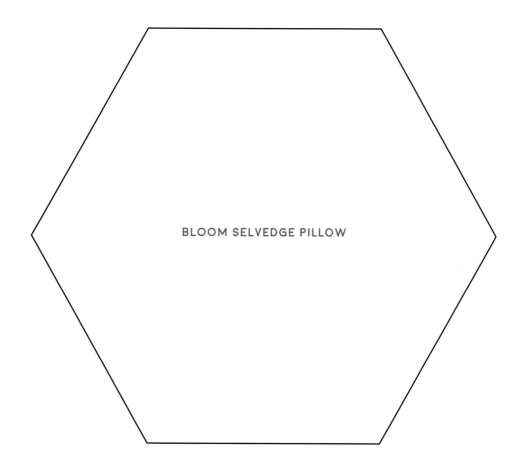

BLOOM SELVEDGE PILLOW

This square should measure 1" (2.5 cm) square when copied.

Index

Contributors

DAISY ASCHEHOUG: warmfolk.com

CHRISTINE BARNES: christinebarnes.com

HEATHER BLACK: quiltachusetts.blogspot.com

ANGELA BOWMAN: angelabowmandesign.com

JEN CARLTON-BAILLY: bettycrockerass.com

LEE CHAPPELL MONROE: maychappell.com

VANESSA CHRISTENSON: vanessachristenson.com

PAMELA COBB: the stitchtvshow.com

ANNMARIE COWLEY: runandsewuilts.wordpress.com

ROSEMARIE DEBOER: quiltingcompany.com

MALKA DUBRAWSKY: stitchindye.com

TARA FAUGHNAN: tarafaughnan.com

JACQUIE GERING: jacquiegering.com

DEBBIE GRIFKA: eschhousequilts.com

VIVIKA HANSEN DENEGRE: quiltingcompany.com

ALLIE HEATH: robertkaufman.com

LINDA HUNGERFORD: flourishingpalms.blogspot.com

GOSIA PAWLOWSKA: quiltsmyway.blogspot.com

SIOBHAN ROGERS: siobhanrogers.com.au

CINDY WIENS: liveacolorfullife.net

SUZY WILLIAMS: suzyquilts.com

METRIC CONVERSION CHART

TO CONVERT	TO	MULTIPLY BY
Inches	Centimeters	2.54
Centimeters	Inches	0.4
Feet	Centimeters	30.5
Centimeters	Feet	0.03
Yards	Meters	0.9
Meters	Yards	1.1

What are you making next?

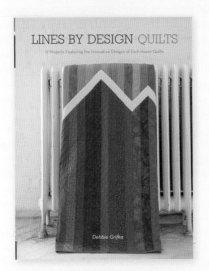